LALITAMBA

2016

Lalitamba ISSN 1930-0662 is published annually in the United States by Chintamani Books. The journal is a member of the Council of Literary Magazines and Presses. Issues are printed in accordance with the Sustainable Forestry Initiative.

Submission Guidelines: Please submit up to five poems or one work of prose (fiction, essay, memoir, interview) per envelope. Include SASE and contact information (name, address, telephone, email). Work should be previously unpublished; we accept first serial rights. Address correspondence to:

Lalitamba
P.O. Box 131
Planetarium Station
New York, NY 10024

Subscriptions are $12 for one year, plus $4.50 postage and handling.

In the Eastern tradition, spiritual seekers don't take personal credit for offering selfless service. A seeker acts as an instrument for the greater good. This is why we don't list staff names on a masthead. The journal is an offering to the immanent and transcendent divine that lives in your heart, and beyond.

Lalitamba, Inc. is a 501(c)3 nonprofit organization. The journal is donated to shelters, hospitals, and prisons throughout the United States. *Lalitamba* also partners with Lalitamba Saranam, a holistic women's shelter in New York City. Proceeds from magazine sales are used for these charitable purposes. Charitable contributions are tax-deductible according to New York State law.

Website: www.lalitamba.com
Facebook: https://www.facebook.com/Lalitamba-252686692751/

The opinions expressed by contributors do not reflect those of the Editor.

The name for the journal was inspired by a *bhajan* sung on a pilgrimage through India.

In early 2004, we traveled through the country with India's beloved "hugging saint" to alleviate the suffering that comes with poverty, illness, and plain loss of hope. The journal was founded upon our return to New York City, in November of that year.

The name "Lalitamba" means Divine Mother. In India, the Divine Mother is also praised as *jagado dharini,* or "She Who Sustains the Universe."

TABLE OF CONTENTS

Essays

Art

LETTERS AND PRAYERS

It only took one man
        to deliver us from darkness
                one God man

And it took Him but four words
                "I Am The Light"

Jim Hart
Brooklyn, NY

LALITAMBA

And I threw everything from me and wandered
toward the East, where the light rises daily. [1]

My life is a letter addressed to the East.
My home is the road from the West to the East.

My knapsack is light; I possess myself.
Thus, I walk—at whose behest?—to the East.

An elephant—white!—plodded through my dreams.
I'm the Buddha? Dolt! Take your jest to the East!

My vigor *vis-à-vis* a monk's is scant.
My backbone is iron. I'm obsessed with the East.

The sun, petulant star, breathes dragon fire.
I, without shame, go undressed to the East.

A hermit wished me Godspeed and said,
"It's done: my long, fruitless quest for the East."

Our common mission in his eyes reposed.
I vowed his name would find rest in the East.

How long have I traveled and what distance?
Surely, it's my lot to be blessed by the East.

My beard is belly-long and millstone gray.
Has the East denied my request for the East?

Joel Allegretti
Fort Lee, NJ

[1] Jung, C.G. *The Red Book*. Trans. Mark Kyburz, John Peck, Sonu Shamdasani. New York: W.W. Norton & Co., 2009.

This journal is an offering.
May all beings be joyful and free.

Ed O'Casey

THE BUTTON THAT SAYS "OFF"

You'll leave the room with the sound of the moon
shattering into a thousand reflections;

it will rain shards of light for days—the tomatoes
will wither and dream of being sown.

Rest against my arm, your pose of resignation;
the grass will bow in a prayer against mowing; unpicked

flowers will dream of the partially living;
soil licks its lips.

I'll lay you down in a borrowed bed and wait
for your eyes to stop twitching—and again

I won't accept your teaching: that I can never love
anything more than anything else;
that I've never actually hated;

that I will only push the feeling aside
and go back to shuddering under a moonless sky.

Ed O'Casey

BLANK ON PURPOSE

no temperature . time
      or light . no consciousness

      but a fading statement
      akin to memory . we were there

           at the birth of light . with the sudden

      vacuum came cold : a place
      in which the sun . had not yet been imagined .

as the gift faded
      into what we could later call . whiteness .

      time flung in all directions . suddenly

           the impact of sense :

      experience starts with a scream

      in a cold room . eventually the discovery :

because it wasn't spooled out
like thread . because it was tossed
into the fabric like a handful of smooth stones :
      everything happens at once :

      the arrogant comebacks .
          the sun in deep fields . the

flattening
                              of love . there's not

enough

            space to contain .

when is decision not a contract with God ?

            the lawyerangels forcing
            signatures . beforeafter time existed .

we are signing the contract . tomorrownow

        to have heads of fire and hands
        of earth . temperature stirs steam

                into water . air sinks back
                                into the lungs .

but not until tomorrow .

        and no later than yesterday .

we are the man in the background
of the magazine cover . shaded
                in a jumble of text .

                    the one blurred at the corners
                    of a coffee stain . it was hot
                            when it dropped .
            now it's room temperature

                    and scalding .
bleach the page and cover our face
in its white . timeless for its impurity.

Lisa Bellamy

QUESTIONS FOR THE ARBORIST

Do you set a regimen of excessive pruning,
or do you accept—even adore—disorder?
Do you think certain species of trees
could be characterized as introverts?
If so, are you gentle?
Are you married? On a scale of 1 to 10,
how would your wife rate your passionate kisses?
Does silence make you nervous?
Do you engage in arboreal foreplay
before you fertilize?
Of man's first disobedience,
of fruit and forbidden trees,
do you have an opinion?
What role does imagination
play in your profession?
Are you comfortable with
the flamboyance of sugar maples?

One night last summer,
the conifer next to the garage
moved several feet away.
Personal altercation or territorial dispute?
No matter. I adopted a *laissez-faire* attitude
toward the new arrangement.
Are you willing to do the same?

If I told you I'm afraid ice jams in the river this winter
could block the trees' flowing *chi*,
would you pledge not to repeat this—
spurting and guffawing—
Friday night at the game and gun club?

Are trees dreamers?

David Swallow, Jr.

THE BLACK HILLS ARE EVERYTHING!

THE WHITE MAN CALLS ME DAVID SWALLOW, JR., but my real name is Wowitan Yuha Mani. I am a TetohLakota of the Wa Naweg'a Band, and I live on the Pine Ridge Indian Reservation in South Dakota.

This is the way my Grandpa Najutala told me, a long time ago. He was a teenager when the 1868 Treaty was signed. He's gone now, but this is how he told me about the sacred Black Hills.

The Black Hills used to be occupied by the Crow Tribe. That was way back, like in the 1700's, even the 1600's. Then, the Black Hills were taken by the Shahiyela (the Cheyenne). Then, the Lakota took them from the Cheyenne. Finally, the white man took them from the Lakota.

The Lakota look at the Black Hills as having spiritual power. All the Plains Tribes look at them that way.

But the white man saw only the yellow rock called gold. They tried to make deals to get the land in the Treaties of 1825, 1851, 1868, and even the Bradley Bill of the 1980's.

However, the only treaty that should be recognized concerning the Black Hills is the Treaty of 1851. At that time, all the tribes signed this treaty, and they signed it in a holy way. The Lakota brought the Sacred White Buffalo Calf *C'anunpa*, the Cheyenne brought their seven sacred arrows, and the Crow, Arikara, and other tribes brought their sacred bundles.

They all held ceremonies before they held the pen. They all agreed that no settlers should enter that sacred area, the Black Hills. The way that treaty was written, this became a non-negotiable matter from that time on. No other treaty would have the right to change that.

But the government and homesteaders, the settlers and prospectors kept invading the Black Hills.

As a result, the Federal Government renegotiated the terms and called it the Fort Laramie 1868 Treaty. This time, the original signers of the 1851 Treaty didn't want to sign. Many were fighting. There were no sacred ceremonies done, and only one sacred *c'anunpa*, only one sacred prayer pipe, was present.

The prospectors and homesteaders brought in whiskey to get many of the signers drunk, so they would sign. My grandfather told me all about this. He saw it, personally. *Mni wakan*, sacred water, is what the Lakota called alcohol, because it affected our people so strongly.

So, this is how we lost the Black Hills.

Six years later, in 1874, General George Armstrong Custer took an expedition into the Black Hills, which included a geologist and numerous miners. What they found immediately caused a major gold rush, and the white settlers and miners began pouring into the Black Hills. The treaties were completely ignored.

In 1876, the Indian Appropriations Act demanded the Sioux give back the Black Hills or starve under siege. Then, they ordered the destruction of all the buffalo herds. By 1889, the Federal Government had forced the Lakota into prisoner-of-war camps, which they now call Reservations. According to government documents, Pine Ridge Indian Reservation is Prisoner of War Camp #344.

Around 1990, I rode seven years with many young people to the Crazy Horse Monument. When we crossed our so-called homelands, we were stopped by the white landowners, because we didn't have their permission. One old homesteader showed us his deed, showing where he had bought the land from the Federal Government. He told us that if we didn't like it, we should go talk to the Federal Government, who got it from the Louisiana Purchase.

So, we lost our Black Hills. Some said we sold them. If so, I believe somebody took the money without any of us Lakota, Dakota, Nakota, Cheyenne or Arikara knowing it. There is no money.

In 1980, the United States Supreme Court said the Black Hills did rightfully belong to the Lakota. They wanted to buy them from us but our People have refused that money. The sacred Black Hills are not for sale.

That's why the Bradley Bill was introduced in 1987 in Congress, to make it look good. It supposedly would have let us live in the Black Hills, while the Federal Government could still mine, trespass, and do whatever they wanted.

Even that was never approved.

So, saying the Black Hills are ours and belong to us are just hollow, empty words. If they are really ours, why can't we live there? They're only occupied by white people with land deeds.

We cannot even go to the Black Hills and exercise our spiritual ways. We are forbidden. We have to get permission from the Government and the BLM, and then we have to follow their rules and regulations. If we are a sovereign nation like they said, we would have our own jurisdiction (county-state-reservation).

If we do still own the Black Hills, we need a new treaty, to re-negotiate a new treaty. All the other treaties were violated or abandoned, often with the approval of Congress, without us knowing about it. That's not supposed to happen in nation-to-nation dealings.

We have a treaty council, a council of elders, all kinds of councils, but none of them are effective. The government and state have kept us hungry and distracted with their projects, which accomplish very little.

Every other foreign nation conquered by the United States has received huge efforts towards rehabilitation and rebuilding. Yet, while the U.S. cries about 20% unemployment, we have 80% unemployment. We remain isolated and have living conditions which are as bad as or worse than any "third world country." Our life expectancy is only 48-years-old for men and 52-years-old for women.

We are the longest prisoners of war in the world's history. It must change. We need to be set free, so we can deal with our own people and our children and their children.

Unfortunately, most of our old people are in the spirit world. Today, our young people have no knowledge of the treaties, the massacre of Wounded Knee, the struggle of Wounded Knee 2, or our history. These are the reasons our culture is dying. No one remembers the language, culture, virtues, or spirituality. No one knows the real history.

But they need to know. If we are to survive, people need to understand. When we're talking about the Black Hills, it's not just the land that was lost but our way of life. It's not just money. Money is the least important thing. We have lost our way of life.

When we talk about the Black Hills, it is about everything. That place is holy and sacred.

Ho he'cetu yelo, I have spoken these words.

B.Z. Niditch

MY CITY NEVER SLEEPS

Nothing,
for a second,
on a side street
dusted with fog,
except the silence
of a somnambulist
carrying a pawned sax
with his sheltered blues
by night-bird haunts,
sweeping woodwinds
into the darkened club
with a cold flashlight
to jam a red eye;
improvisation breaks out,
shielding all sights,
as budding sounds
from unfinished songs
finger open
a furtive hour,
tangled with mystery
embedded in lips
burning like piles
of coal and fire.

B.Z. Niditch

DROPPING EVERYTHING

In Memoriam, Denise Levertov

Your words
are here
never lost
or turned off
or back
to back
always drawing
near and ready
for recognition,
leafing through
the mind's eye
to ask for
your thoughts
on peace,
even by the ounce
or to weigh in
a sudden answer·
from a labyrinth
of new sun glasses
turning over
your muted lenses
at first light
on frozen windows
along charred
drifts of permafrost
as the black cat
near the daily paper
speaks of war
and scratches over

LALITAMBA

the snowy steps,
you, Denise Levertov
quickly inhale
the air's vibration
and drop everything
on grounds
for peace.

Kathleen Gunton

INTERWEAVING A.R. AMMONS:
CENTO

Falling into sleep, dream, dream and
You can climb, climb
The universe with its
Interweaving.
I started to look out thinking
Plenty around for the mind to dwell on: that's a comfort
For a moderate life and a safe death.
Sanctuary, sanctuary, I say it over and over and the
Shadows are bodiless shapes, yet they have a song.
Water, like spirit, jostling hard stuff around
In a still diversity of completion.
The saints are gathering at the real,
The most beautiful haunting
Inner silence
Throughout the universe.
I've made it this far.

Source: *Collected Poems 1951-1971*

Simm Landres

PUT A PEBBLE

Kiss the marble
put a pebble

a stone a rock
from scree

if not enough
a boulder then

think flotsam
much debris

but not flowers
decorations

shrivel and do shrink
to flaccid stalks

and stink as vegetation
smears the ground

succumbs absorbed
and melts down

kiss the marble
put a pebble

minerals abide

Jim Hart

THE ROOTS OF OUR MOTHER'S GARDEN

On August 4th
the date of her eldest son's birth
she died

The sun shone
birds sang
summer boys played ball
summer girls skipped rope

Fruit
ripened on vines
hung from branches

People
went to work
vacationed
stayed home with real and conveniently imagined illnesses

Men and women
older than she
gazed out their windows
onto worlds that still included them

Waves crashed the shores
as for millions of years

Desperation shook me silent
contemplating the immensity of what should be said

On August 4th
the date of her eldest son's birth
she died

Leaving me
at 45
an orphan

The sky darkened
briefly
or at least I thought it so

The desire to break something
curse someone
deny God his existence
grew like Mary's rage
watching Her only begotten son hanging on the cross

Every great loss
should be measured so

On August 4th
in the middle of her eightieth year
Elizabeth Rita Batson Hart
slipped
with the same quiet dignity and grace
she displayed in life
into death

Worrying more
I'm sure
about how her "boys" were taking it

Robert Kostuck

THE ASCENSION

LUZ STANDS AMID THE BRUSH OF SOFT WINGS, the distant rhythm of whirlwinds and tornadoes.

A crumpled paper bag, wind-loosed from a doorway of bottles, cigarette stubs, and a discarded Los Posadas *luminaria*, blows against her ankle, then bounces off and away down Central Avenue in the direction of the river.

Piety envelops her.

Sunday afternoon—a dirty city, a filthy world; one might wish for the best and anticipate the worst.

This morning, Father Muñoz says, "Petition the Lord, yet wait not for an answer."

Luz's brother Cruz says, "He means get off your butt and work. Isn't that what I'm doing? What petition, anyway?"

Luz's soon-to-be sister-in-law Ramona glares and pinches her fiancé's hand. "A little humility please."

Petition? Luz prays twice a day, sometimes more. Work? At seventeen? She's headed to the restaurant, right now. Humility? Her scarred face taught her humility; pride, forever a stranger to her thoughts.

Each day seems beautiful, when you are ugly and left to walk alone to work on a cold morning, the thermometer at thirty-four degrees and the sidewalks empty. Who walks anyway?

If only she owned a car, or better yet, were loved by a boyfriend with a car—like Savannah with her rich white boyfriend.

Impossible.

New Mexico's brittle gray air sweeps little brown leaves onto the sidewalk.

"THIS THIN BLOUSE and itty-bitty sweater don't make it," says Savannah at the restaurant. "It's freezing, and I'll be here half the day. You should use the alley door, anyway. "You smell that?" she continues. "Julio burned something in the kitchen. Baby, you look all shivery. You ready to get dirty?"

"It's not so bad," says Luz. "There's worse things."

"You're working with Hector, today. Can you keep up with him? He's a spry old man, don't you think?"

"Spry? What's that?"

"Lively. Full of life. For an old man of forty at least."

Savannah unlocks and re-locks the door, sweeping in the wind.

Santiago enters, nods hello to the two girls, and rushes to the kitchen.

"Hey you," says Savannah. "Yeah you. Use the alley door. I mean, you know that, right? You're working with me, Santiago. Try to stay focused on your work, okay?"

Turning to Luz, she says, "If I catch him staring at me with those big eyes, I tell you—I don't know what I'll do. What will I do?"

"What will you do?" says Luz.

Savannah looks down at the top of the reception desk and wipes a laminated menu. "Don't you two go to the same school?"

"Cesar Chavez Community School over on Palomas. It's a charter school north of Gibson."

"You know, Baby, if you used a little eyeliner, something for that pretty smile—Ever try? Here." She reaches beneath the counter for a tube of cherry-flavored coral-colored beeswax-based lip gloss.

Luz slips it into her pocket.

The girls walk slowly, as they approach the kitchen.

Luz ties on a red apron over black slacks and white Peter Pan collar blouse.

Mr. Walsh unlocks the door exactly at noon, and two waiting families hustle in, shivering.

By one o'clock all the tables are full. Customers wait in the foyer.

Hector takes the orders and delivers the meals.

Luz removes plates of half-eaten food, the dirty cups, and silverware. She wipes down the tables and rushes to reset the tables with paper placemats, napkins, Tabasco sauce, ketchup, salt, and pepper.

In the kitchen she helps Julio rinse cutlery and dishes. She dumps out full bowls of salsa and sets her plastic dish tray next to the sink.

"What the heck is that?" says Julio.

"A diaper." Luz says, staring, as surprised as he is.

"Who would put a diaper on the table, change a baby in the same place people eat, and leave the poop for me to clean up?"

She drops the stinking mess into a waste barrel in the center of the kitchen.

"No, no," says Bill, "take that outside. "No human waste in my kitchen. Give me a break. Use this plastic bag. Put that plate under the sink. I'll disinfect it later."

Luz remembers to wash her hands. The water pouring off her fingers and wrists takes on a silvery sheen.

THE LAST OF THE FLATTENED BOXES tossed into the dumpster catches on its edge. Santiago leans over to loosen the cardboard and shove it down.

Right at that moment, Mr. Walsh slams open the back alley door. "Kid, what're you doing? How long does it take to empty the trash? No dumpster diving while you're on duty. Hurry up and get your sorry brown butt back in here. Come on. I ain't gonna hold the door."

Santiago's seventeen. He knows when to shut up.

The door bangs shut.

Santiago returns to the kitchen, ties on his red apron, and pushes a greasy dish cart into the restaurant.

Savannah serves and steps behind the cash register counter. With her teased hair and makeup, she's as pretty as a pop star.

Mr. Walsh steps up, his hand brushing her skirt's gaudy ruffles, his chin resting on her bare shoulder.

She drops change, so that some of it misses the customer's outstretched hand and falls onto the floor.

On Sundays the restaurant closes at five. Mr. Walsh grabs a handful of receipts and shuts his office door.

From across the room, Santiago tries flirting with Savannah, his words a hesitant murmur.

"We need to find you a girlfriend," says Savannah.

Julio and Hector step out for cigarettes.

Luz imagines a boyfriend's gifts of polished turquoise set into silver; gold rings and earrings; copper bracelets, seashell necklaces, and glass pendants. Jade. Ruby. Topaz. Garnet. Emerald. Amethyst.

Then, she feels feverish, hot with penitential flames. Maybe she's getting sick—the flu, food poisoning, a virus.

She follows Savannah to the kitchen alcove, where they hang their coats.

Mr. Walsh is right there, stepping past them, his fat body blocking the back door. "I'm going to Santa Fe this weekend. My suppliers up there are always trying to cheat me on every damn deal. What I do is check into a nice motel for a couple of days. That's deductible, and I get my business done. All work and no play is no good, so I try to have a little fun. I try to relax, with no wife and kids for a few days." He stares straight at Savannah.

"Excuse me, Mr. Walsh. My ride is waiting."

"What are you talking about, Chiquita? This is an opportunity for us to get to know each other better, and all you got to say is 'Excuse me'?"

Hector comes in from the front, and Julio bangs a ladle against the big soup pot. The clanging is enough to distract Mr. Walsh.

Savannah slips out the door like a rabbit.

The latch clicks, and Mr. Walsh dents his own metal door, kicking it open.

Savannah is already seated in a mud-spattered Jeep, with her blond boyfriend from the university.

"I gave you this job. I was going to make you hostess— ungrateful, stupid—You're fired. Don't you even think of showing your face around here!"

"F— you, f— you!" shouts Savannah; and to Luz, "Baby, remember what I told you."

The Jeep squeals out of the alley onto Girard Boulevard.

Mr. Walsh turns to the rest of them in the doorway and says, "What the f— are you looking at?" He shoves Santiago against the wall on his way into the restaurant and pauses long enough to glare at Luz. "You're not worth looking at."

Santiago is shaking all over. He is ashamed, frightened by the big man.

Mr. Walsh is gone.

Hector pushes through the swinging doors into the restaurant.

Luz cries quietly.

Julio watches the two teenagers.

"Hey kid, you walk Luz home, okay? Do that, *amigo*," Hector says.

Santiago pulls on his jacket and holds the door for Luz.

She isn't pretty like Savannah, and she has that pink and white scar on her face, with more scars on her shoulder and arm. Her hair is long, parted in the middle.

As they walk, she pulls the hairband from her ponytail and lets darkness cascade over the sides of her face. She runs her hand up under her hair, fingertips testing the skin.

Santiago knows. Girls are mysterious creatures. Words tangle in his mouth. He feels excited and satisfied, just walking with her.

This is enough, until she leans into him. The back of her left hand drifts across the back of his right hand. He is astounded to feel their hands slip together, touch, and curl into something new and undiscovered.

They walk the half mile to her house on Santa Clara Avenue without talking.

She smiles, and he lets go of her hand on the sidewalk in front of her house.

Forgetting everything her sister Tina told her, she lets it happen, makes it happen, quickly kisses him on the mouth.

He smiles like the sun.

"Thanks for walking me home."

Side by side, they stroll up the cement walk to the door.

Her mother is waiting, cotton apron thin, dishtowel in hand, hair pulled back into a tangled bun. She peeks over her glasses. "Who are you?"

"Santiago, Mama. He walked me home."

"Young man, thank you. Now, you get in here, Luz."

"Thanks again. See you tomorrow at school."

"I'll be there," he says.

BOTH OF LUZ'S PARENTS are at home as usual on this Sunday afternoon, her father in his chair watching sports on television, her brother Cruz visiting with his girlfriend Ramona. Father and son watch the soccer ball go back and forth. Mother, Ramona, and Tina prepare a big dinner in the kitchen.

Home aromas soothe Luz's scars. The reality of cold streets and noisy restaurants is forgotten.

The women make *enchiladas*. Luz stirs the sauce. The kitchen is warm from the oven.

"Young men walking young ladies home," says her mother. "You don't see that anymore, and when you do it's a nice surprise." Her words bounce off of the kitchen's yellow walls.

Luz steadies the pot on the stovetop. She holds the handle tight, so that there are no spills. Her entire body feels sinuous, flexible, lit with tiny orange flames.

Ramona knows right away.

"Head in the clouds? Hey ladies, I think Miss Luz has a boyfriend. That boy who walked you as far as the front door? Not ready to meet the father face to face? Yes, yes, I knew it. What's his name?"

"Who? What?" Luz blushes, stirs the sauce.

Mother peers into a bowl, tacitly ignoring the young women.

"His name," says Ramona. "The handsome young man who walked you home. Or are you sworn to secrecy?"

The women laugh, assess the sparks flowing from the girl's fingertips, from her hair.

"Santiago," says Luz, "but he's only a boy I work with. We go to the same school. What are you staring at?"

The teasing feels good, the women without men.

Ramona winks and nudges Tina.

"Your little sister's growing up."

"Do you mean Linda Estrada's boy?" says her mother, "That Santiago?"

Luz stares at her hand, amazed by the lingering sensations. She touches her fingers to her lips. Ramona and Tina smile.

"Yes," says Luz. "He's the one."

IN THE DREAM THAT NIGHT she is enveloped with light, cold wind, and the flutter of a million wings.

On the edge of the stove is a pot.

Her mother glances away, and Luz reaches up for the black handle.

Boiling water scalds the side of her face, splashes onto her shoulder and arm, soaks her pink butterfly blouse. Half-boiled eggs fall onto the floor and smash. They steam and singe, spilling creamy yoke.

Which are louder—Luz's screams or her mother's? Their two voices are sirens in the yellow kitchen.

Outside, an ice-cream truck plays a scratchy loop of "Take Me Out to the Ball Game."

Luz hears the sound of neighborhood shouts. Somewhere, a driver shifts gears, and a bus lumbers down Central Avenue.

Luz begins to shriek, as life continues outside the door.

She foresees something of the meanness and hopelessness of life: Middle school, awful. Quinceañera, a white gown against her dead skin. High school, no prom date. The teasing and staring, endless. The city, one of distorting funhouse mirrors.

Years pass, and it all comes true.

Father Muñoz interprets her sadness as vanity. He attests to a faith that embraces miracles, but his words intended to soothe are forgotten aphorisms from *Ars Moriendi*. He smells of incense and beeswax, of moldy books and starched chasuble.

Luz intentionally ignores his words of comfort.

She tells no one of her prayers for a miracle. She thinks of St. Barbara's promises, St. Cecilia's sweet song, St. Bernadette's visions.

Every day now for years, the words have remained unchanged, everlastingly repeated. "Torment," she prays, "release me from my pain and shame. If I am your example of the foolishness of vanity, yet I practice an utmost humility. I have served. I petition you, please embrace me."

LUZ WAKES, SWEAT DRIPPING from her temples, moisture pooling between her breasts. She kicks back the covers and rests her palms on the cotton shift over her belly.

He's a sensitive boy with naïve brown eyes, and always in need of a haircut.

Then, she remembers Santiago staring at Savannah's round bottom in tight jeans.

Savannah, Miss Popularity, done with high school and taking classes at the University of New Mexico. She is three years older than Luz.

It might as well be thirty years between them.

Who will take Savannah's place in the restaurant? she wonders, thinking of Mr. Walsh's onion breath, his hand sliding down a girl's hip and squeezing.

Her red scars turn pink in the sunlight coming through the window, her long dark hair a curtain against the horrible faces of the world. Yesterday, the shouting and swearing; the banging pots and pans; Mr. Walsh cursing and kicking the door; Santiago shoved into the wall. A terrible life.

What will Savannah do without a job? She lives with her boyfriend, the blond guy in the jeep. Ricky? Rocky? Rodney? Luz can't remember the name.

She imagines a boy, near and warm. The thought makes her face hot.

Santiago, Santiago. Her blanket slides to the floor. The cool air wisps in from tiny cracks in the window, an Arctic whisper. She directs her attention to his many possible hands, smiles, voices.

A mystery unfolds—a night flower's tight corolla, extended stamens, bee's breath, pollen rain. Flowers sprout up, blossom above her breastbone, and shower perfume across the bed.

MONDAY MORNING BRINGS winter rain. Albuquerque goes gray with seasons of accumulated debris.

The city falls into the wet arms of sadness. Overnight, well-intentioned citizens have developed minor illnesses—sore throats, ragged coughs, congestion, muscle aches, lethargy. Now, bus riders are sluggish and pedestrians, distraught. Cars and trucks cut through rainbow-slick puddles.

Luz wakes shivering, her skin like ice on a summer day, her fever slight.

Her mother feels Luz's forehead, measures her pulse, peers into and around her eyes, and makes two phone calls.

"I don't know what it is, but it's going around. Stay home, I think. If it gets worse, I'll think about taking you to see a doctor. Probably only a cold. Anything special at school today? I'll call in for you, now. One more blanket—You must stay warm. I'll be right back."

"Mom? I don't feel too bad. Maybe I could try to go to school?"

"I'll make you some hot tea, okay?"

"And some Saltines, like you used to do when I was a kid? But then, I think—"

"Let's decide in a half-hour." Her mother walks off to the yellow kitchen.

The temperature of Luz's room fluctuates between too hot and too cold. Her body shakes without flu or virus, cough or muscle aches.

Thirty minutes later, she waits at the bus stop.

Santiago is standing there, silent.

They ride the bus for eight miles, the sweat in chill trickles across Luz's warm body.

CESAR CHAVEZ COMMUNITY SCHOOL. Language Arts, first period. Santiago sits in the row of desks beneath the windows.

The two lovers stare at each other long enough for others to notice. Hesitant whispers circulate.

Luz casually applies the cherry-flavored coral-colored beeswax-based lip gloss Savannah has given her.

All day, she moves through the few classrooms for English, science, and the weekly art class. Boys sense her awakened body and find reasons to stand near her, to speak to her.

She instigates small talk with Santiago.

At lunch, know-it-all girls stare, wondering. They converse so that she can hear, an invitation to participate. They want information. They re-appraise gawky Santiago, analyze him from what little they can divine.

Esme, the most popular girl and the meanest, intentionally bumps into Luz. "Oh, did I step on someone? I didn't even see you there. You kinda blend in with the wall, easy to overlook and everything. So sorry." Esme turns her back to Luz and elaborately brushes her hair, courting girls and boys alike.

Her jealous snub makes the boys look harder at Luz, as if trying to see past the surface of her eyes.

"I'll walk you home again," says Santiago, and the lunchroom comes to a minute of pure silence, a penitential stillness in the silliness of adolescent discovery. The children perceive possibilities beyond the narrow confines of the moment, see themselves as adults, parents, adventurers, and explorers. They are witnesses to grace and passion.

THE RIO GRANDE POURS THROUGH ice-age canyons. Strong river, cold wind. Yellow-brown cottonwood leaves revolve in eddies. Brown water roils—the endless curlicues of sediment spiraling, dissolving, reforming. Spring struggles up from under New Mexico's ice age. Tree limbs waver, suggesting purple and yellow buds. Red-tailed hawks part the day.

Walking from the bus stop, Santiago and Luz hold hands.

He dares to put his arm around her.

She acquiesces.

Thick winter clouds fill a random sky. A breeze, scattered raindrops, a sudden sheet of cold water.

Running to her house on Santa Clara, they pause on the porch, away from door and windows, embrace and kiss. A moment passes. The moment lingers. Maybe for thirty seconds, though it might as well be thirty years.

Both are shaking, and the light grows suddenly clear, warming a large pile of adobe bricks that may or may not be used to build a house of many rooms.

With the sound of the chain lock, Luz's mother appears at the door.

Luz and Santiago spring apart, once again becoming two.

Luz sees that her mother sees and understands. Her mother turns, returns with an umbrella, and casually offers it to Santiago.

"Return the umbrella another day," she says, dismissing him. The three of them speak proper parting words.

Luz and her mother watch Santiago walk away. The rain is pensive with words left unsaid.

"Come in, now. How do you feel? Go change. Get into bed. I'll get the thermometer, and I'll make us some hot chocolate. Or would you like tea?"

Mother and daughter sit in a dim room, not talking. The light is grey, this rain the precursor of another season. The rain washes away dirt and grime, sins and guilt.

Luz wears a white shift and sits wrapped in a colorful blanket. The hot chocolate is warm, sweet, and seductive.

The thunderstorm ends, passing east.

Her mother falls into a dreamless sleep.

Luz feels the fire inside, flames curling up from within her, filling her belly, her torso, her arms and legs.

Butterflies, moths, dragonflies, cicadas, wasps, fireflies, and bees fill the room. They whisper encouragement to her.

The world—a crisp cold day with tight, low-angled afternoon sun. Above her, clouds depart, leaving a pale seamless blue.

The colorful blanket slides to the ground. Luz steps out of the house and down from the porch.

Albuquerque is as still as ice. She hears the gurgle of flowing water, nearby.

Santiago is waiting, shivering. He steps out from under the wet leaf canopy of a desert ironwood tree. Its leaves are constantly unfolding, for the tree is an evergreen, bright and wet in the preternatural light.

Who shall believe?

Maybe Father Muñoz will believe. Maybe Luz's mother and father will believe. Maybe their faith will be enough.

Piety. Humility. They envelop Luz's fervent desire.

The iridescent insects swarm, discrete squadrons of sound and vibration.

Luz feels the coolness of the air as she rises, joined by nighthawks, curve-billed thrashers, cactus wrens, gnat-catchers, black-throated sparrows; a great spiral of translucent and feathered wings gliding, guiding, growing into a silent pillar of light.

Ayaz Daryl Nielsen

SOPHIA'S CROCKPOT

at the ending, sigh
from within self-tolerant mangrove
from within suddenness in time
from within magical African rain
from within crow and night crawler
from within fly, grub and bacterium
from within caravan, catamaran and canoe
from within Marrakech, meringue and salsa
from within rain shadow of mountain
from within twilight alpenglow
from within hidden moon
from within angel, demon and *dakini*
from within sea gull windsurfing
from within murmur of forgotten language
from within Paris sunset lime tree
from within All Ways

always always always
from within maggot

sighing exhalation of
gazillionths brilliant ingredients
everything

pulsating archetype of endless creation

Marilyn Joy

LETTER TO SANDRA CISNEROS: HOW HER STORIES SET LOOSE THE STORY OF ME

"But I began then to think of time as
having a shape, something you could see,
like a series of liquid transparencies,
one laid on top of the other."

—Margaret Atwood, *Cat's Eye*

Dear Sandra,

As I opened your books
I watched the words fly from each page,
like children from a schoolhouse
on the first day of summer, like
candy flung from a pink *piñata*—
then angry, as rocks aimed with intent,

as gunshots from an angry mob,
dissidents from a landscape
of convention, of a predictable life, neat,
tied-up, invisible.
Anarchy found me,
followed me into my living, caught

in my throat, crept into my dreams,
and I had to tell you, tell you how they
came to form my story, a story
forgotten, disenfranchised,
tucked in a drawer—an old sweater
waiting for winter when

the earth teeters quick and bare, and there
is nowhere to hide.
That's how it came to me—through
the space between your words,
a breath between a sentence, my history
undone inside me until

there was no more room, and
it had to find its sanction,
its softness, its ruthlessness in the world.
And I saw it was a good life, a story
not unlike your own—
at times tenuous, tender, willful.

◆ ◆ ◆

So it began that I came to America,
crossing the other border, north
into a country also grown from
the restlessness of men, of
those seeking freedoms not of their land.
On prairies, mountains, bowls

of granite and green
they stood, claiming ground
that had never needed tenure nor title to
those that knew its distance
and possibility—this endless sky
and flat horizon, extremes

of hot and cold beyond ideas
my grandparents would know,
this hard ground that rose up hard men
and even hardier women;
my mother's mother speaking French—
not as evidence of refinement,

for her tongue was trained that way to
survive a day—though that
language abandoned her
the night her father left them on the steps
of St. Augustine's—a sister, a brother;
her father, so reconciled to loss

when his wife died
that he gave them to God, to the righteous
will of the sisterhood
where her fingers, manners, and mind
were trained in that convent—
a custodian of abstinence and prayer

that taught her how to
crochet exquisite doilies of lace
and later to make babies, more than nine—
one stillborn and one
to die beneath a train in his brash youth.
Such burdens

born of a woman's mortal sin, for
tempting man,
for bringing disobedience
into the garden of Eden—a disobedience
my grandmother would
never claim until the end of her life.

♦ ♦ ♦

My father's mother was widowed young
from a farmer who
left her five sons, a daughter, and
the endless toil
of dearth and fifty acres on her own.
Thought by most as odd and aloof in her

love of painting, an art made
for the luxury of time and freedom
a poor prairie woman could not afford,
yet she painted people and landscapes on
hand-stretched linen with oil—
pigment pink for summer roses

brushed on loose satin
with money better spent on necessities.
Her life, as steely and sharp-edged
as the palette knife she had
never been trained to use, hard and sharp
like the land she was bound to.

♦ ♦ ♦

My mother danced soft-shoe, jive, swing,
and waltz, practiced in the kitchen,
on the porch, at Saturday night dance parties,
and taught the children of neighbors
what was lent to her legs for such pleasure,
and took payment in potatoes or

a barter that would justify her
time away from chores.
When she wasn't stirring a breeze
with her body, she was stirring her mind, for
she loved to read: historical fiction,
true romance, Sears and Roebuck catalogue,

anything her eyes could lift from the page
into her imagination.
The eldest of nine, no time to
dream of English royalty,
the sovereign cast in her novels,
or dream of dances that would make

life lighter than what she knew,
so she married the youngest son of
that farmer's widow.
He played the fiddle at local gatherings,
was as handsome as Clark Gable,
and danced—and loved her dancing.

Ah, into those long Canadian summer nights,
where on the window of their youth
they wed, moved to that farmhouse
already full of his family—four brothers,
a young sister, his mother, stern and peculiar—
silent brooders all.

Her life—crowded, mislaid in this frugal house
of fatherless men, of weighted women.
Add to this a child, a boy
who four years later
would pull me, his baby sister, in his wagon,
where she would come to see,

with censure and despair, that the life
she thought she had left behind
had found her on this remote landscape of
responsibility; had weighted too
her once light-stepping husband,
had put aside his fiddle, his love of dance,

had callused his heart, until
he was loathe to work the land
that broke the spirit and added little
to the family pocket, had made him question
his life, his courage to step out of it—
to find a way to make it his own.

◆ ◆ ◆

So he left his wife and baby boy in
the care of his mother, left
the yellow grasses of low-lying horizon,
the hard blue sky,
for a ground grown in swelling rolls
of pine-scented green, that wore the sky

on its head and held you in the shadow of
its timbered stature
in those far woods of northwest territory,
Inuit Indian home,
shared a tent
with one old Native of this land

to save money for
my mother and brother's passage,
traded labor with a woodsman for the
use of a one-room cabin—
a box nailed to its rough exterior,
his refrigerator,

and no outhouse. (It would be his barter
to build a double-seater
and repair the roof of the cabin.)
This was where I, too, was made—from
my father's joy to have his
wife and son with him;

born on the eve of winter, on the edge
of a river, in
the twilight of a forest, in
an evergreen pocket of British Columbia;
no grandmothers or cousins, aunts or
uncles to show me

what we carried with us from the prairie,
to slow my father's restlessness north,
where as an infant, unaware of
the lines men draw
to separate themselves,
I could not question this movement away

from what was known, past that northern
reach into what was unknown—
a vast Alaskan Territory, a possession,
not yet a part of—
held at arm's length
by the neighbor to the south needing

able-bodied men to ready its furthest fences
around this frozen tundra—
young Canadian men to join the war effort;
offering a uniform, training,
a green card at the end of enlistment, and
the certainty of food and shelter for family

at a time when certainty was scant
and Alaska still untamed territory, wild
with possibility, a straw taken
in the hopefulness of a moment. Yet
did the northern reach of long twilight days
make my childhood memories faint,

dreamlike, where snow was dirt, was street,
was playground, and even air
and life looked black and white, like
the pictures in our photo album.
My father's discontent as dark as the days,
my mother's strength spent looking

for the light
that could lift their poverty of heart.
More than four years
before the darkness would send us south,
more than four years
leaning against what wanted to move—

what would become
a legacy of movement throughout my life,
that sent us searching
for what was
thought to be lost,
for what had never been given,

for what might be discovered, be found
somewhere other than
where we were,
momentum that would carry us across this
unseen border
into America—into

◆ ◆ ◆

a land of sea and sand, of palm trees and
warmth, of light only dreamed of,
into a California that knew
my secret longing for sun—for
a Technicolor state of plenty, a state
long and drawn of mountains and deserts,

coastlines cut by a blue-green spread,
ever south across
another unmarked border—
these unexpected threads
winding in around and through one another
forming the cloth of my future—

the green card, my Aunt Eve's
Canadian undoing (marrying a soldier from
the land of milk and honey),
writing letters of sunshine, surf, and jobs…
wish you were here, and
so we were.

Or, it could have been
the fire that burned all our belongings—my
favorite brown bear, the doll
my aunt gave me for my third birthday—that
sent us south into the sun.
I did not care for reasons, did not

cry for Alaska, for those gray days and green
woods of my beginnings.
I could only stare in wonder at the long row
of palms lining Ocean Boulevard—
sparse and straight,
dusting the sky with tassels of fringed grasses;

leaves like nothing a mind could imagine,
their bodies, brown stalks
anchored between the sidewalk and street—
the street as wide as a runway,
with my eyes intent at
the edge of the car window,

at the edge of my uncle's '44 Chevy sedan.
I was no longer on planet Earth.
I was on planet Light—on planet Sun,
feet anchored firm
for the roiling surf in an ocean that was warm,
in an ocean that could carry you on a froth

of white momentum for the shore; for the hot
sand that sends you
running for a blanket, digging for shells to line
your windowsill—for
castles and motes of foam, for
dreams of sea creatures and sailboats,

for breathing the deep, moist salt
of this new home that I thought would
be different, that I thought
would leave what was behind—this shroud
of snow softening in memory,
lifting its heavy cloak for the bright sun,

a sun that lays sharp shadows, like the ones
you carry in your bags as you move
from place to place, that don't burn in a fire
or melt in the spring with your departure,
that live inside your heart, not as retribution
or reminder, but for their redemption.

◆ ◆ ◆

So we moved into
that small basement apartment, three miles
from the Port of Long Beach,
oil derricks on nearby Signal Hill, their
steady whoosh and groan
heard even in the night—

iron grasshoppers that stole the air,
that pumped out their stench and stained
the earth with
their black spill of progress that
became a curiosity,
a forbidden playground.

Like scouts for an ant colony
our journey south
forged a path for family to follow,
their suitcases standing at the door: two
grandmothers, one grandfather,
an uncle, and my mother's

sixteen-year-old delinquent sister.
They loved the sun, too
and loved the family that would
fasten them to it, would feed and shelter
their discouragement.
All lived with us at one time or another,

most in succession.
Once, three at a time—seven
in a one-and-a-half-bedroom duplex,
the half being
a storage room where
my brother and I shared a bunk bed.

I don't know where they slept—the sofa,
the floor, the bathtub?
A blessing, a curse,
our family's constant migration,
leaving my memory as confused and
crowded as our living room,

and my recollections of life appear to be
measured from this passage, from
the dark into the light, light
that lets you see
more of yourself,
not necessarily what you want it to see.

◆ ◆ ◆

I'm told I was a child as strange and secretive
as my prairie-painting grandmother,
as obedient as the other one
forged by the fire of a nun's hand, and as
dramatic as my mother's
unfulfilled ambition as a dancer,

as cautious with my pen as my father with
his heart—forever wanting
to silence the doubt,
this unruly tenant inside his head;
yet there were gifts, too
from this ground that gave me into myself,

that lifted its seed in the only way it knew,
that loved what grew
from inside itself, because of what it was,
gifts embedded in this child—
her life leaning in on me like a dark night,
like a well wanting water,

her value and influence so misunderstood.
I tried to eradicate
the roots, to still the momentum
of a mind made
from this dim beginning, where
to this end, mercifully, I did not succeed.

Thus, this is but a chapter in
the book of me, or maybe but a sentence.
Or could it be the whole story,
embedded between
the lines of my childhood?
A misplaced map for life,

looked at once again because of
what you wrote, Sandra:
books with stories not unlike my own,
quiet humanity evangelized
through life in its most mundane moments.
Fingers to find binding after binding,

tales and talebearers, heroes
from the most unlikely beginnings flying
from their assigned space on the shelf,
set loose by a knowing wind
from a far off prairie, from the thick woods
of my birth, from the frozen subsoil

that left me clinging to the sun;
wind lifting each character from the page,
from the close corner of words—
a conversation with strangers
who knew confusion, too
but did not run from it, did not scold it and

even spoke of a beauty in its bewilderment,
in the wake of its sigh.
The anarchy of life was their paint, was
the ink inside the carefully formed letters
of their story.
What wonder to find my thoughts, feelings,

my family, my mistakes
were not new,
not tragic, not what I
had made of them—these villains and heroes
all but the pen of the author;
the disowned and ordinary finding

a new home, quite extraordinary between
the pages of a novel, a memoir,
historical fiction—weft of
the same cloth—the voice, part truth,
part imagination, part madness…as is life.
You told me this, Sandra,

when I met you on *Mango Street*,
followed you and your stories across
Woman Hollering Creek
into your *Wicked Wicked Ways* with poetry.
Your accent—part Chicago, part
Chicana, layered the lives

of your characters
with such ease, such attitude, such sorrow
it broke loose the cup
that held my own history;
reading of the lawlessness, the pain,
the restlessness and romance,

even the pettiness that
was made tender by your pen.
I found myself over and over in each line.
These were stories to steal away old ideas
of how life looks,
giving failure and loneliness a new face,

less maudlin and encumbering;
your voice, without edges, dipping in and
out of English,
fascinating yet unfamiliar words
laced inside the language—confident,
unpredictable, startling!

A tongue tasting of *masa*,
the heat of *habaneros*,
eyes watching without knowing, without
the certainty of what would be there,
that this life might become
something new under your pen—

colorful threads woven into fabric,
apparel for a dark day, for a revolution!
The quick and slow words
I thought I knew,
that didn't follow these rules I
had been taught, that

had their own mind, direction, duration,
that stood defiant, yielding—
each amending
into the truth of the moment,
a self-satisfied dialect
that made me

want to find my own way, to speak with
my own vocabulary and rules
that I brought with me as a child
moving across these
invisible borders of county and province,
territory and state.

◆ ◆ ◆

I watched you weave characters
that didn't apologize or eulogize the life plot
they had been born to.
They galloped and sprawled across pages
with little punctuation or respect
for the rules of a language they didn't invite or

invent—that could slow their
brash or timid arrival into a world said to be
both predictable and uncertain,
and too often unkind
for *Salvador Late or Early*, who broke my heart
with his... *body too small to contain*

the hundred balloons of happiness,
and the... *Texas girl who smells like corn, like*
Frito Bandito chips, like tortillas,
Lucy who wears aqua flip-flops,
who asks, *Have you ever eated dog food? I have,*
and Cleofilas Enriqueta DeLeon Hernandes,

who finally found her voice in laughter...
gurgling out of her own throat,
a long ribbon of laughter like water.
Through each page,
its gray-black print, the even lines, the unlikely
characters, I entered your life and

you mine, without the arbitrary ideas of origin,
of politics, of language.
We came together
carrying sadness and surprise in our pockets,
to meet ourselves, to honor
our histories without shame or apology or

embellishment that might
hide the sweetness and strength in us,
more than we had known before.
And so I thank you, Sandra,
for inciting mutiny in me
that will not leave me rest in that safe language,

in that safe space of knowing
what comes next, in writing or in life,
for not hiding between these comfortable
lines and quips about characters
that never held breath in this spinning world
that knows of no beginning or end—

only ordinary middles,
and the stories
that seep from their wounds and their wonder.

Kathy French

SHARING THE INN

In the scant shelter of a December
doorway, she and her belongings are gathered
like a bouquet. Her Asian bones are
wrapped in crocheted pink, purple, and red,
her own elegant handwork.

Draped over all is a plaid jacket.
She receives food, blankets, hot tea,
refuses a sleeping bag;
at night she crawls under black plastic.

Daily, we talk near the park.
Reeking of urine and filth,
she is beautiful, through and through.

I consider warnings against strangers
and Christ's mother needing shelter in the barn.
Finally, I invite, and hesitantly she accepts
the sanctuary of my home.

My children and grandchild recoil.
My landlord calls the police.
Many consider her dirty, foreign, criminal—
but strangers are friends not yet known.

My friend is dying, and she dies.
In her last week, she curls tenderly
against me like a newborn.

"Your second birth day is coming," I say.
We laugh and weep, nearly collapsing
in the joy of knowing each other.

After she dies, she returns in a dream.
Smiling, she offers her satchel,
"For your journey."

Kelly Jadon

HE CALLED ME HOPELESS

All my life I looked
for where I belonged.
The judge called me hopeless.
After I finished doing time in the Arizona desert,
he gave me just one year in the county;
I thought he'd sentence me to life.

Out West no one could see me,
no local eyes phoning mom.
There was no shame,
so I embraced addiction
and became the "Ho."
I told myself,
Either you'll get over this
or die.

They called me an honest crackhead,
because when I got back, mom sent me to
Sunday School.
I didn't belong there, either.
On the street corner
the bailiff would pick me up.
He knew my way home.

My folks deemed me incorrigible;
they locked me up at 14,
though I had committed no crime.
The judge kept me on "probation."
Afterward,
I dropped out of school.
The army brought out my lost self,
and I moved up the ranks,
as a leader.

As a kid, I spent freedom
sitting amid pines
wondering,
What's my purpose?
Today, I can't blame others
for most of my life—
those skeletal years.

I will no longer utter,
If only.
I've accepted my situation,
put aside my anger,
learned how to break
ties and curses,

forgiven.

I can be strong.
I've learned to trust.
I go back behind
gates, fences, bars, and walls
to those still inside

who suffer with shame,
who believe the lie,
You're hopeless.

Larry E. Graham

PRISONS

MOM IS EIGHTY-NINE. She lies on her bed in the living room and watches the morning news. She's mostly in the silent stage now, but once in a while, she speaks. This morning she says, "Those Russians, on the move again."

I'm having a doughnut fantasy—a chocolate cake doughnut with nuts on the top, and a cup of coffee. Strong coffee.

She says, "We should have bombed them when we had the chance, before they got to Berlin. That's what Dad says."

I've told her before that Dad died years ago, but she always talks about him in the present tense, so I don't say anything, anymore.

I hear something. Voices.

I step to the window and lift one of the blinds a quarter of an inch, just enough so I can see my neighbor without him seeing me. He's working on his bar bike, one of those motorcycles with the handlebars higher than the rider's shoulders.

I try to avoid my neighbor. He wears his Nazi helmet everywhere, even while working on his bike. He has tattoos on his face, chains on his boots, and a pony tail that hangs past his shoulders. And he's a racist.

His girlfriend, the one with arms like slabs of beef, the one sitting on the upside-down bucket chatting with him, is worse than he is. Every sentence she utters contains epithets of one kind or another.

I say, "Mom, I'm going to pop over to the doughnut shop. You want a doughnut?"

Mom doesn't answer. She's staring at the screen.

I pull the belts over her and strap her in. Not too tightly, just enough to keep her in the bed.

I take the back door out, because it's on the side of the house that faces away from my neighbor, and hurry down the block to Franklin Boulevard.

The woman behind the counter bags my doughnuts, and I'm ready to go; but the coffee smells so good that I decide to take a couple extra minutes.

"A cup of coffee and another chocolate cake with nuts," I tell her.

I'm stirring the creamer into the coffee, when I hear the motorcycle. My neighbor dismounts and clumps into the shop.

"Look at 'em," he sneers, pointing back at the men who stand outside the doughnut shop in the morning, waiting for someone to drive up and offer them work.

"There's only two kinds of 'em, y'know."

I'm sure there are more than two kinds of guys who wait at the doughnut shop for someone to offer them work, but I don't say anything. I have to watch what I say around my neighbor.

"There's the young ones who just got here," he says. "All they want is a car and flashy clothes and a blonde girlfriend. That's all they want."

"I see."

"The others," my neighbor continues, "they've been here a long time. They have families in Mexico, but can't visit 'em, because it's harder to get back and forth across the border, now. They're stuck. They have to stay here. They have to work and send money back to the old lady. That's all they can do. They're like prisoners."

"Really."

"Serves 'em right," says my neighbor, "for taking our jobs."

He takes his doughnuts, jumps onto his motorcycle, and roars away. He always seems in a hurry, though I've never heard he has a job, or does anything else on a schedule. I can look over at his house any time of the day and night and see him moving around, doing I don't know what. Maybe he's writing a novel or something, writing day and night. I don't ask what he does.

As soon as he's out of sight, blasting down Franklin Boulevard, terrorizing the other drivers, I take my doughnuts and coffee outside. I stand beside the men waiting for work.

I say good morning to the man next to me, a short fellow about twenty years old.

He smiles and says, "Gooth more-nee." Then, he returns to his conversation with the other men waiting for work.

Like them, I stare across the parking lot at the traffic on Franklin Boulevard. I listen to their Spanish, hoping to pick up a few words to add to my vocabulary. I've been trying for years to learn Spanish. Maybe, one of these days I'll be able to sign up for a class at the City College.

An older man, a guy with a gray Zapata moustache and a sweat-stained cowboy hat, suddenly speaks English. "Betty," he says. "Good morning, Betty."

Betty approaches from the rear of the doughnut shop. She may be thirty or thirty-five years old, and would be attractive if she didn't carry the marks of the street life. Deeply sunburned skin. Copper-colored hair matted against her head. Dirt beneath the fingernails.

Still, you can see she's attractive. You can see that, and it's disconcerting.

"Carlos," she says, her voice hoarse. She turns her head aside and coughs briefly. "My friend."

"It's good to see you today, Betty," Carlos says.

"And you're full of crap today, Carlos."

Betty, Carlos, and the others chuckle. When Betty steps into the doughnut shop, one of the young men says in Spanish, "I'd like a little of that—if you hosed it down, first."

The men laugh, but Carlos shushes them.

Betty has come out of the shop, already. She doesn't speak Spanish, so she couldn't have understood them, but Carlos shushes them, anyway.

He says, "Haven't seen you for a while, Betty."

"Been on a run," she says. Her hands shake, as she holds the coffee to her lips.

"On a run? I didn't know you are a runner. To where do you run?"

"Don't know," says Betty. "This happens sometimes, you know. Yesterday, I woke up by the river. Don't know how I got there. Had the worst shakes of my life."

"Sorry, Betty." Carlos sips his own coffee and looks toward Franklin Boulevard.

Betty blows on her coffee to cool it. She holds two fingers to her mouth. "Don't got a cigarette, do you?"

Carlos quickly brings a pack from his coat pocket.

Betty takes two. "One for later?" she says. "That okay?" She pockets the second cigarette.

Carlos holds his lighter to the cigarette between her lips.

She draws in the smoke. "And you couldn't loan me a buck, could you? I got a friend coming over, today. I'll pay you back."

"That's okay," says Carlos. He reaches into his pocket and hands her a five. The other men scowl at each other, then roll their eyes and smile. Carlos says, "I have a daughter of your age."

"I know," says Betty. "You told me." She sips again, and draws on the cigarette. "You tell me every time I see you."

"So," says Carlos. "How is your family? How are the kids?"

Betty shakes her head. "Don't know. Haven't seen them." She looks into his eyes, and her own eyes seem to redden and swell. She wipes a sleeve across her nose. "You don't know what it's like, Carlos, when you can't see your babies. They're growing. You know? Every day they're changing, but I can't see them. The county won't let me."

"I'm sorry, Betty," says Carlos.

"Can't even call them on the phone."

"Yes. I'm sorry."

"At least you can call your family on the phone, right? At least you can do that."

Carlos doesn't answer. He looks away, his face flushing.

Betty sighs and grinds the cigarette beneath her shoe. "I have to go, now," she says, in tears. She turns away, and in a moment she's gone, behind the doughnut shop, the way she came.

One of the young men puts his hand on the other's shoulder. He speaks in a squeaky voice. "I yam so sore-ee, Bettee."

Both men close their eyes, throw their heads back, and laugh.

Carlos growls at them, "Shut up. Shut the f— up."

The traffic on Franklin Boulevard is heavier, now.

The men at the doughnut shop will get work, soon. Most of the passing pickups carry material for the day's work.

I watch them go by—a truck loaded with two-by-fours for a framing job, another truck with long black-and-white pipes for a plumbing job, another with cartons of roofing shingles to be nailed to someone's roof.

A pickup loaded with trowels, bull floats, and shovels, and towing a concrete ready-mix trailer, pulls into the parking lot. It stops at the side of the doughnut shop.

"Dose home-bras," says the driver, and two young men scramble into the cab.

That's when I remember Mom. I don't walk back—I run.

By the time I get back, I'm gasping for breath. Inside, I find Mom struggling against the straps. She's frantic.

"Where were you?" she cries. "I thought you left me."

"I left for just a minute. See? I went to the doughnut shop. I got us some doughnuts."

"Don't ever leave me, Dad. Don't ever go away again. I worry so much about you. I worry. Don't you love me? Tell me where you were. Where did you go?"

Richard Alan Bunch

UNDRESSING THE SUN

In this journey of fools
with their lists

of ought and must,
poets can still sling out a song

about loneliness shown
by another's chimney

as a branch goes over the falls,
hope to be lost

in a motionless light,
carol about a voice in every wind,

seek elegance as they
undress the sun,

note white lightning and
haunted streams,

and find in ancient dreams
a miracle born

as they toast with a
glass brimming with
visions and the
seas of God.

Madonna
Kathleen Gunton

Indian Offering Bowl

W. F. Lantry

THE SOURCE OF LIGHT

I once possessed, a little while ago,
or had in my possession for some time,
a small statue of Mary standing in
a lotus blossom, carved from ivory.
Perhaps the craftsman meant to sculpt Kuan Yin,
compassionate, serene, joyful, sublime;
and overcome by bliss, forgot all those

shared figures, symbols, signs: the way her clothes
billow in streams, her necklaces, her hair,
her long ribbons flowing in sacred streams,
as if the vortex of her harmony
spun everything around: this earth, our dreams;
until her transformations became prayer
in our own voices, incantations heard

as universes in a single word.
And as that word replaced a thousand signs,
the sculptor left them out, although she stood
within a lotus still, her ecstasy
mirrored by petals, as if blossoms could
alone become her signature, where lines
converge in prisms, meld, and start to glow.

Guy R. Beining

PLANETARY BUZZ

He heard the hum
of steel & her skirt
sliding down the banister
& nightfall expanded
& lamps blossomed,
falling on lacquered bodies.
Vessels passed
under bridges
& birds with crystal toes
stood atop snowdrifts.
The city lights merged
with the breath of stars
that took away
all dark places.

Munich/Germany
Sarah Katharina Kayß

Matt Schumacher

BOY WHISPERING THE STARS
TO A WHITE HORSE

A
boy
goes looking for
the missing eye of the white
horse that crosses a pasture to
greet him every morning. He
would like nothing more than
to reward the pure kindness of
the horse   and return the eye
to its rightful owner.

and
reveals
the endless
visions of its eye, which has seen things
no one
on the planet can begin
to imagine, having
traveled to the end
of
the
uni
verse...

He looks for the eye of the white horse in the waterlilies
of ponds, in emerald pastures, under waterfalls and in
snowy meadows, hiding in the fragrant blooms of wildflowers.
He cannot find it anywhere. The search is arduous, but the boy
does not grow discouraged.   He looks until, out of the corner
of his eye, he begins to catch the sparkle of the horse's eye.
It is a faraway star, ineffably beautiful, like the   beginning
of the   endlessly unknown.   And, one evening, across a
the boy   whispers

barbed wire   fence,
to the   far
horse   in a   but
from   country   language   can both
that horse   under
the   of
and   man   stand,
the   do not   know.
stars,

Thomas Penn Johnson

THE DOUGHNUTS

"DO YOU WANT SOME DOUGHNUTS?" the white boy says to his dark-skinned friend, who has joined him on the porch.

It is a bright, almost hot, April morning. Both friends are young, and their blood is on the rise.

"Because if you do, I got a powerful urge for some doughnuts this fine Saturday mornin'. Yep, powerful! Apple and spice, or maybe a couple of them right out of the oven, glazed ones. Yep, that's the ticket. Whaddaya say, Bossman? Don'tcha think we oughta start this fine spring mornin' off with some of Mister Ike's doughnuts?"

"Now, I want to tell you somethin', boy," the dark-skinned boy starts in. "When it comes to a-wantin' doughnuts, you got to recognize who you're talkin' to. First of all, I grew up in Winston-Salem and used to stop in regular at the original Krispy Kreme Bakery, nearly every Saturday night after I left the show at the Lincoln Theatre. Yessir, so you ain't comin' in at the head of the class on this one, brother.

"Shucks, I almost got my butt whipped over some doughnuts when I was eight years old. My mother's boyfriend had the nerve to ask me private-like if I wanted anythin' while he was out romancin' my mother, so I told him, 'Sure, bring me some doughnuts.' I didn't know the guy was goin' to remember to bring the doggone doughnuts. He did, and he told my mother they was for "that chocolate drop" of hers. My mother wanted to kill me, but I got me some doughnuts out of the deal, and I'll say this. Ike's doughnuts right out of the oven will put Krispy Kreme's to shame.

"Now, how do you propose we get way over there to Ike's place to get these doughnuts, this fine Saturday before Easter Sunday?"

Neither of the two men owns a car or holds a driver's license. Neither is employed. Twenty years separate them in age, though they have been friends long enough for the friendship to take hold.

"Well," says the white boy, "I think it's somethin' we need to do, so let's get the mo-jo goin' here and find us a car."

"And who's goin' to drive this car, mister-I-ain't-got-no-driver's-license-white-boy? Naw, what we need is Jimmy's Galaxy 500 settin' right there in front of us. We just go upstairs and get the keys, and away we go."

"There's the ticket," says the white boy.

Jimmy, an eighteen year old white boy, is sleeping soundly on the dark-skinned boy's bed. He likes to sleep there. No one has ever before asked Jimmy to loan out his car keys, but this doesn't matter to the homeless adolescent, after he awakens to the soft calling of his name.

"Jimmy, Jimmy," the dark-skinned boy calls. "Jimmy, I'm takin' your car keys to go get some doughnuts."

Still groggy, Jimmy closes his eyes again and says, "Wake me up in time for us to..." Jimmy doesn't want to talk right now. He's falling back asleep.

"For us to what?" asks the dark-skinned boy.

"You know," mutters Jimmy as he drifts off again.

WITH NARY A CARE, THE TWO FRIENDS enjoy the long drive down Genesee Street. There could be nothing better to do on a lovely spring morning—the sun bright and a serious blue overhead—than to be riding together in a 1968 Galaxy 500 to obtain some of what are generally known to be the best doughnuts this side of Paradise.

The young know by instinct, the old by bitter experience, that life doesn't offer many better moments. It is no fault of the Almighty that we humans are always looking for something less simple to content ourselves.

The dark-skinned boy is at the wheel.

About a mile from Ike's Bakery, the two friends come up behind a car being driven in a dilatory manner. The tentative driver pulls nearly to a stop over towards the left, as if to make a left turn, so the dark-skinned boy tries to pass on the right, even though Genesee is a two-lane road.

Instead of turning left, the car turns right and smashes into the side of Jimmy's car.

It is unmistakably clear that this is quite a fine mess the two friends have gotten themselves into. Before he gets out of the car to face the music, the dark-skinned boy says to the white boy, "Look, there's no point in us both goin' down over this. Why don't you skedaddle on back and let Jimmy know what's happenin'. I'll talk to these people."

The white boy is agreeable.

Only then does the dark-skinned boy get out of the car. He doesn't turn around or stop walking, until he turns off of Genesee onto Locust Street, about a mile away.

He is hardcore independent in his thought and ways. He's a conservative radical in politics, and sometimes he is out-and-out radical in the way he dresses. Today, he is wearing tight-fitting leather pants and a worn jean jacket with the sleeves cut off.

The middle-aged white lady who emerges from the other car is visibly disconcerted, when she sees the dark-skinned boy approaching her.

Her two sons, aged ten and eleven, have exited the car from the passenger side. The two sons, standing for a better view of the approaching boy, are instantly mesmerized. Their eyes widen with delight, and when the dark-skinned boy comes to a halt before the family of three, now gathered close together, he cannot evade their glances.

"Ma'am, here's the thing. I'm a Christian, and I hope you are too. You, see, ma'am, I'm in trouble here. I don't have a driver's license, so I don't want to report this accident to the police. There's practically no damage, ma'am. Do you think we could work somethin' out between us?"

The two sons move in closer to their mother. Their eyes dart anxiously back and forth between the two adults.

They watch their mother's eyes survey the street before she makes a judicious response.

"Well, I try to be a Christian person...but I just don't know," she says. "Maybe I ought to call my husband first." She hesitates, furrowing her brow, still not sure what exactly she should do, then looks alert and continues, "Maybe I should just call the police."

"Call Dad," her oldest boy suggests.

"No, son," she says, "I want you to go over to that store—" She points to a small grocery store nearby. In front of the store, a clerk and a few customers have gathered to watch the negotiations. "—And ask someone to call the police."

Neither hesitating nor flinching, her son rears up and stoutly replies, "No."

His mother is flabbergasted. Her son's defiance is uncharacteristic. She can tell by the look in his eyes, a look she has never seen before, that her boy has thrown in entirely with the dark-skinned stranger.

Smarting from this public desertion by one of her ever-dutiful sons, she looks to her younger son for wonted filial obedience, whereupon he steps closer to his brother and demands, "Call Dad."

And so, pliant like one who has been stunned senseless, the mother leaves her boys in the custody of their new-found ally and ambles over to the grocery store to call her husband.

There in the street, two white sons and a dark-skinned boy stand silently together, smiling at one another, their bond maturing into deeper friendship.

The white sons, the dark-skinned boy, and all the circumambient spectators then notice a city black-and-white pull to a stop behind Jimmy's car.

The dark-skinned boy's first thought is that the officer will turn out to be his nemesis, Officer Shirley, which means that he is going downtown, notwithstanding what his friends' father says to their mother, as would be any of his friends were they present.

The dark-skinned boy is astounded to see instead a cop he has never seen before emerge from the police car—a white cop, most definitely a white boy, young and fair, yellow-haired with the look of an Olympian athlete.

When the officer approaches the dark-skinned boy and his new boon companions, the dark-skinned boy says to him, "I'm goin' to tell you straight out, Officer. I got myself a problem here."

"You don't have a driver's license," the officer says.

The officer and the dark-skinned boy simultaneously break into a smile.

In a spirited refrain the two brothers answer, "Right."

They all become aware that the white boy cop has thrown in entirely with this ironbound friendship, this subtle brotherhood, here established on a public thoroughfare. They are like Yoruba tribesmen discovering by the language they speak that they have happened upon each other, in a land far distant from their several homes. They are like strangers partnered in a high stakes card game who discover, when the game begins, that they are so fluent and precise in the language of the eyes that their opponents will be incapable of detecting or prevailing against them.

To the delight of the dark-skinned boy and his two young friends, everything turns out exactly as they desire. No written report is to be filed. The matter will be left to the parties to settle. The white lady's husband promises to contact the dark-skinned boy by phone, if he determines further action is warranted, but for the moment he's satisfied with his eldest son's unreserved assessment that the damage is negligible.

All participants and spectators take leave of the scene. They know that they will never speak to each other or see each other again.

The dark-skinned boy aims to come back later with Jimmy to pick up the car.

ARRIVING BACK AT HIS HOUSE, the dark-skinned boy finds sitting on his stoop the self-same white boy with whom he began the day.

The white boy says, "Dang. I ain't been here twenty minutes. Must be some kind of record."

The dark-skinned boy shrugs his shoulders and says, "Just one of those things."

The white boy adds, "I tole Jimmy 'bout the accident. He wanted to know if you were all right, and that's all he said. Just rolled over and went back to sleep."

Awake but still in bed, Jimmy is waiting for his friend.

The dark-skinned boy opens the door to the bedroom. He figures he must start with a sincere apology for damaging his friend's car, but Jimmy speaks first.

"Did you get the doughnuts?"

"I stopped in at Markey's Grill on the way home. They buy their doughnuts from Ike's Bakery."

Brian Phillip Whalen

RISE

MY FRIEND ERIK TAUGHT ME how to make a challah-like bread.

"There are different recipes," he said. "You'll learn to make your own adjustments."

Our *boule* was plump and taut, the shape of a starving child's belly.

"Before we braid," said Erik, "tell me how we got here."

"First, we ran the tap, until the water was lukewarm; then, we measured one-and-a-half cups into a mixing bowl; we added a quarter cup of honey, plus one tablespoon of yeast; then, we whisked; next, we added a quarter cup of powdered milk, two eggs, and two cups high-gluten flour; we whisked again, and when the mixture held the consistency of glue, we scraped the edges of the bowl; we covered the bowl with a damp kitchen towel and set it in the oven for forty-five minutes."

I tell him this and ask, "The pilot light will warm the glue?"

"The glue," Erik corrected, "is called a sponge."

"When the sponge doubles, remove it from the oven; the yeast should be well active, the mixture bubbling and popping like a mud spa; the sponge will smell like beer; drizzle a third cup canola oil over the surface of the sponge, and sprinkle one tablespoon sea salt over the oil; using a spatula, fold the oil and the salt into the sponge (about ten strokes, vigorous); when the mixture is uniform, add three cups flour, folding the mixture with the spatula until the flour is incorporated and a soft dough forms; drop the dough onto the counter, dust with flour, and knead; work the dough until it feels smooth and elastic—like an earlobe—adding flour when necessary; tear off a piece of the dough, stretch it between your fingertips, and hold it to the light: if it resembles the wing of a bat, the dough is ready to rise."

"And if it doesn't resemble the wing of a bat?"

"Keep kneading."

Haya Pomrenze

THINGS THAT MAKE THE FITZPATRICKS THINK WE'RE CRAZY

Reading Hebrew right to left, starting at the back of the book.
Riding up and down on Sabbath elevators,
  stopping at every floor.
Swinging chickens over our heads for Kapores
  on Yom Kippur Eve.
Throwing challah into the lake on Rosh Hashanah,
  next to Joe who caught a grouper.
Playing "Jew or Not Jew."
  Kate Middleton, Madeleine Albright, Julio Iglesias: Jew.
  Not Jew: Tim Geithner, Orlando Bloom, Dennis Miller.
Asking a Shabbos *goy* to turn on a light, turn off a stove.
Eating and sleeping in palm frond huts,
  ceilings decorated with X-mas lights.
Walking to *shul* in 90 degree heat, in a thunderstorm,
  or in the snow—there and back.
Telling everyone we're half, three-fourths, or fully Jewish.
Saying no to cheeseburgers.

Elizabeth Moller

THE STUFF WE DON'T SAY

[It] is the great taboo…White folks fear their unspoken views will be deemed
racist. People of colour are filled with sorrow and rage at unrighted wrongs.

—Eva Paterson

It starts as a moment in time.
Like this:
One of Your children is shot.
In his pocket is a pack of candy, warm with palm sweat.
It is February 26th, 7:30p.m., 2012.
The police have his body, with his Skittles, his iced tea, his cell phone.

For a short time, the five hours before they release him, the police also have his killer.

Before [the verdict], there might have been some confusion
or uncertainty as to how evil a state or judicial system
could be, how blind a jury could be…But after that, it was
really, really clear that we are prisoners of war.

—Philip Agnew

Fourteen months later, the watchman is back in police custody, against his will and theirs, at the demand of a special state prosecutor.

A year after that, a jury is selected; the trial begins.

◆ ◆ ◆

In a month he is free.

◆ ◆ ◆

Juror B37, talking to the silver fox newsman, describes the killing as "an unfortunate incident that happened."

She says there were riots after the shooting; there were none.

She says the killer's "heart was in the right place."

Our communities are occupied by a police force that kills, that profiles and is deputizing citizens and allowing them to treat poor people and people of color the same way.

—Philip Agnew

I, with the pale skin of my ancestors, did not expect this verdict. You—you, lower case, singular: you did.

I live in Harlem. The next morning, when I walk outside, I stand for a moment on the stoop of my house. *My* house.

Not so long ago, it was home to squatters and addicts.

Meanwhile, *you* are not part of the physical and present You, walking past me now.

And I wonder if this walking mass of You is thinking about It. I wonder if You hate Us, as I imagine I might, in a tables-turned world.

But, NO, my friend Jenny says. NO. There is no You, no Us, no We. It is a construct that we must look past and through. She considers herself one of You, so don't put words in her mouth. Don't confuse her with Us. Jenny serves the marginalized. She has a degree in social work. She has creamy skin and freckles.

It is all a construct.

Jenny does not feel guilty or responsible. She does not feel compelled to talk about It *ad nauseum* with anyone who will listen, no matter the subsequent and awkward silences. She works with poor people.

It is a construct.

But no one has ever called the police on her, fearful of her fire-truck red hair. No vigilante watchman—"displaced by the vandalism in the neighborhood and wanting to catch these people so badly" (Juror B37)—has ever leapt out of his car to chase her seventeen-year old unarmed son down the street before shooting him dead. 99 to 1 odds no one ever will.

But, anyway, she says, there is nothing of value we can add. It has all been said, already. She is exasperated with me.

Juror B37 does not hesitate to speak up, as if the jury's ambassador, as if to speak for them all, as if to speak for the rest of Us.

It is all over the news, but It is not to be raised in polite circles. We don't like the dark and strained conversation.

And so, We don't talk about It.

Drowning in silence, we are brothers and sisters drowning each other.

—Eva Paterson

Of course, We are not a monolith.

Some among Us don't talk about It, because We don't know what to believe. We don't have all the information, yet. When We sort through It all, then We'll talk. We promise.

Mostly, We talk about things that We can more or less agree on and make sense of, right now, in this moment, in Our City that We live in.

Others of Us don't live among You, and We truly don't think about It at all. When We must, It is an artificial conversation forced upon Us by the talking heads.

Some of Us don't talk about It, because We fear riots. A revolution. Just look at Egypt. There are still people in the streets there, risking their lives, their children's lives. Some people want justice, whatever the cost.

We saw those chalk signs on the sidewalk. (We pretended not to.) We fear for the safety of Our children.

◆ ◆ ◆

It occurs to some of Us (as it must to many of You) that some of Your children are locked up for much lesser offenses than taking away a boy's breath: Five years for slashed tires in Texas. Sixteen for an $11 (armed) robbery in Mississippi.

We look at Your little boy next to Ours on the swing set, pumping legs high and free to the trees and clouds. Our eyes sting, and we try to stop thinking about It, to look beyond the construct.

◆ ◆ ◆

But He looked suspicious, some among Us say. His sweatshirt had a hood, and he was wearing it. There had been break-ins. Not that night, no. But before. Our window glass had been shattered.

And It was legal. You must respect the Law. What will protect Us, if not the Law? It was a jury of Our peers, after all.

◆ ◆ ◆

Mostly, though, We don't talk about It, because We don't have to.

Also, some of Us don't believe that It happened like that. That has never happened to Us.

We are at once both invisible—in the helpful way, the way that doesn't attract unwanted attention—and markedly visible. No one is more visible. They sound a frantic alarm when Our children go missing (and not just the autistic ones).

That is not Our fault, We say.

◆ ◆ ◆

Still, some of Us are apologetic. Deferential. "Sorry, sorry, sorry," We say inside Our heads, to no one and everyone. We are so sorry about It all, so sorry that It has come to this.

We have been touched in that soft place, the place that only music reaches.

◆ ◆ ◆

Then, We (accidentally) cut one of You off at a subway turnstile, and You glare. You are reading too much into It, We think. We are not being rude to You. We are rude people.

And why shouldn't We be? We have been taught that, in this City, aggression gets Us: A seat on the bus. A free cup of Joe. Jobs at Our law firms and publishing houses. Bargain buys. The bartender's attention.

◆ ◆ ◆

Our aggression—or rather, "efficiency"—is different than Yours; it gets Us into Princeton.

It is not Our fault.

So, with that in mind, You are the one being rude, now.

But, then.

We wonder. Maybe We misinterpreted Your look. Maybe it wasn't a glare after all. Or maybe it was a glare, but one unrelated to Us. Maybe We are the ones reading into things.

We don't know what to think. We don't know what to do.

What can We do? We change the cat litter, hauling Our large garbage bags of animal crap and piss out onto the street. We scrub Our hands clean—first with soap and water, and then with Our all-American, turbo-germ-killing hand sanitizer, rubbing it all over, between palms and into finger nooks.

◆ ◆ ◆

We worry that You hate Us, and that prospect makes Us feel ugly inside.

We try not to think about It.

We hope that You aren't thinking about It.

We are scared of You.

◆ ◆ ◆

Some of Us don't talk about It, because It's too hard to talk about without taking action, and We are too busy to take action. We have Our families to think about. We have to make money, put bread on Our table.

We are stretched thin as a cobweb, as it is: Colicky infants. Toddlers on the autism spectrum. Teenagers who cut (forearms) and pull (hair). Temples throbbing with gas bills, school loans, the mortgage on the house. Bosses who call Us on Our cell phones at all hours. Spats with Our wives. (We never have sex anymore.) Single friends who complain. (We have fallen out of touch.)

They demand, and deplete, and then fade away. We are alone at last, but it has not worked out the way We expected.

We have terrible lower back pain, tendinitis in Our knees, stage IIIC testicular cancer.

Also, Our parents are dying.

When not stuck in those muddles, We just want to take a load off, and watch a sitcom, or crack jokes, or spout nonsense at Our local watering hole. Is not this one of Our inalienable rights— the pursuit of happiness? All We are asking for is the freedom to drink, laugh, and get happy. You would do the same thing, if You were in Our shoes. Anyone would.

◆ ◆ ◆

Some of Us do talk about It, but only when drunk or high, or in that wonderful place We call Abroad, when We are asked about Our problems. We answer in a broken foreign tongue.

◆ ◆ ◆

A mother sporting bright green skinny jeans with six zippers and a black tank top asks You about Your child's hair. Your daughter's head rests on Your knee. With each of Your answers comes another question.

We see on Your face that there has been an intrusion. We pretend not to hear.

We don't want to be that mother, embarrassing Us all.

◆ ◆ ◆

We fear that if We talk, out will come the shovels and the magnifying glasses, and the many hypocritical pockets of Our lives will be unearthed and displayed for all to see, World Fair style: The way We ask You to help Us at CVS. The way We neglect to say hello, though We see You every day. The way We allow Our children to meander serpentine down the sidewalk, so that no one else can pass, while You snap Yours to attention to make room. (But that is what they teach Us!, We protest, Our early childhood development experts…) The way We are oblivious to Our spatial footprint. (Fog-headedness won't cost Our children their lives.) The way We fail to recognize You, though We've met on multiple occasions. The way We sauntered up to one of You that time and said, "Hey, girl." (Where did that come from?)

◆ ◆ ◆

There are things that We want to ask You.

But We fear.

We fear that We will use the wrong words.

And then, Our question will hang mid-air, a balloon expiring in infamy.

◆ ◆ ◆

Our children are asking Us questions that We don't know how to answer.

We imagine Yours are doing the same. Maybe You have the answers.

How can We explain to Our children what We choose to ignore?

◆ ◆ ◆

We tell Our teenagers not to walk down that street on the way home.

"Why not?"

"We need to be careful."

"I am careful. I'm always careful."

Our children aren't listening to Us.

But life goes on down here below,
And all us mortals struggle so.

—Steve Earle

We are relieved, when We find Ourselves thinking about It a little bit less. The signs come down from the windows. Crisp air moves in on the subway platform, and the clog of human sweat disperses.

The leaves are changing.

◆ ◆ ◆

Can't You see that everything is just fine, now?
Please don't hurt Us.
Forgive Us Our sins and the sins of those before Us.

◆ ◆ ◆

We overhear Our child use that word. He thinks We're not listening. Our chest goes hard.

"Where did you learn that?!" We shout at him.

He must have learned it on the streets, We tell Ourselves, and later Our friend, over two bottles of wine.

"I don't know."

"Where?"

But he won't tell Us, says he doesn't remember.

Not even Our children will talk to Us about It now.

◆ ◆ ◆

it is hard to breathe the still silent air without choking it back up, and so i go to you. my skin is pale, yours warm and brown. you, my friend, therapist, substitute mother. i ask you about it.

you say: a cold sweat shocked me out of sleep. it was the middle of the night, but i was compelled to pick up the phone. i called my twenty-year old to tell him what to wear: fitted jeans. shirt tucked-in. more importantly, what not to wear: jeans slung low. a hoodie

you say: you know something is wrong. why do you not speak?

i don't know how. i write you a love letter.

i told him (you say) not to run when chased. not to fight when attacked. but i don't know whether that will be enough (you say). i am scared (you say). i feel alone.

me too, i say. please don't leave.

Z.G. Tomaszewski

SUMMER AFTERNOON

Perched on a birch
        hummingbird holds repose

in the stalled clutches of its green wings.
        The bird's undercarriage

heaves white,
        paint scraped against bark.

There's something in this world
        that slows us

no matter who you are.
        Say, for example,

the scarlet stop sign
        of the poisonberries

or the deflated tires
        of your lungs

exhausted from running
        or the idle engine

of the oil-hot sun
        weighing a heavy brake

on the vessel of the body,
        the vehicle that is this earth.

Gloria Dyc

WHAT COULD HAVE BEEN

1.
"What could have been—"

I was on top: in candle light. We looked at my undulating shadow cast on the wall.

"What is," I wanted to say but couldn't.

The next day he went to his *pueblo* for a feast and I to the hot springs in Ojo Caliente.

"Let's not fall in love. It wouldn't be traditional," he said the first time he placed his hand over mine.

I bathed in the mineral waters, a sacred place for the native tribes, and later bled profusely.

"Come back. I'll be no later than 8:30p.m."

I drove back to the house in Lamy. Lights out, no car. I drove around. An hour later, he returned, closing the gate to the driveway.

"I'm glad you waited," he said, tying his robe. He sounded ambivalent. Did he want to sleep with a bottle of Scotch?

I bled again, that night. I knew what might have been could no longer be. The starched white sheets were ruined.

He rolled them up, vexed. He was on a grant to write in a house awarded for residency. I often wondered whether he tried to wash the sheets or just threw them out.

The next day, he broke our date to see Dylan in Albuquerque.

"I have so much work, so much to do."

Eyes tearing, I carried my bags out. He escorted me to an apricot tree, picking fruit as if that could be enough. This was more a "poetic moment" than an act of contrition. Ignorance.

GOD...I cried all the way back home. I held onto him the way a primate holds onto a dead infant.

Delusion. I clung to what was dear. He was the Bird of Paradise, speaking carefully, spreading his brilliant feathers. He told me once, after our first embrace, "Some say I'm the best they ever had." He climbed women like vines. I cringe, looking back at the years of attachment. Insanity!

2.
When he came into my life the first time, he said, "Let's not fall in love. It's not traditional. Control is possible in the Realm of the Gods. I don't want any more children."

He placed his hand on mine while talking, then put it back on the wheel. At Chaco Canyon he leaned against a wall. In the sun, the precision: He spread his arms and legs. He looked like a DaVinci drawing. He alluded to the misdeeds of the *pueblo* and the persistent drought. I never pressed for more. Now, I think I understand.

"I don't know crap," he said once. When he wanted to meet here or there, between his travels and readings, he warned me every time, "If you don't, I have others who will..."

I pass the De Anza, a now defunct hotel on Central Avenue, where I arrived first and ended up paying for the room, and I think of him.

"I was a star, as usual," he said that night, taking a flask of liquor from his jacket pocket. He was an animal.

3.

A decade later, I received several letters from Arizona. He had been sober for a few years. I had become a mother and tried to be a partner to my son's father: a rodeo man and dreamer who listened to Rush Limbaugh.

Hopeless, hopeless, hopeless. "Your mother is getting old," he told my son before he abandoned us for a younger woman with a house in horse country along the Rio Grande.

After two chaste years, I invited the Bird of Paradise back into my life. Again, he said, "What could have been…"

We met and shared a room for the Modern Language Association Conference, staged in New Orleans. He avoided me by day: I am not tribal. I have no totems. He had areas to prepare and dances to perform.

I teach five classes of first and second year native students. An indigenous colleague said, "I like you, because you walk with the people."

One night, we were in heat. The fluorescent lights of a strip joint were blinking onto the bedsheets. People walked past our room laughing, and we didn't care. We were lost—in each other, in what was.

I didn't ask the next night why I wasn't invited to dinner. I shopped around town and bought a voodoo doll. He picked up the paper bag and said, "It's alive," and it was.

"You just want sex. You don't want to really be with me." I was vitriolic, as he took his morning pleasure a few hours before his plane would leave.

"Food for thought," he said. "Take care of yourself." But I didn't. Delusion.

4.
When he came through town, I'd be around. If he wanted to meet, I found a way. I wore him like Christ wore the thorns around his heart in those "holy" pictures.

He hooked up with a clique of elites. Another woman? Of course. They traveled around the world talking critical theory to dozens around tables. Profound. He invited me to a hotel in Albuquerque, greeted me shirtless, and turned so I could see the deep gauge of her nails. Why couldn't I accept that what could have been wasn't, and never would be?

Because of the way we held each other's gaze. Because of the way he blurted out, "I belong here," my dark earth tight around his man root. Because of the way his tears wet my face.

"Am I a dirty old man?" he'd ask. His hair was whitening, his body scarred from brawls and accidents.

We shared extra flesh in the middle, the softening of burning candles. He ran his hand along my side, over my hip. "Your skin is so soft. If I were a sculptor, I imagine how I would create you."

"What could have been"…was.

5.

On our last night together, we were kicked out of a hotel for making too much noise. I dragged him into a vintage clothing store. I bought a pair of four-inch heels: black, Italian. I laughed as we walked to the car. At times, I needed to lean on him.

"You can't lean on me all the time." He was perturbed.

At the hotel, I placed the shoes next to the TV set. Before he slipped away in the morning, he lifted them up and said, "Maybe next time."

There was no next time. I called him out. "So, are you going to Europe with your post-modern, deconstructed theorists traumatized by 'otherness?'" (*ha ha*)

He wrote, "All points of connection between us have been spent. Or many, most."

I gave up. Months passed. I sent pictures from my phone and brief updates. He drove by my house once, honked his horn, and fled.

For a year I lived on one grain of hope, as the Buddha had lived on one grain of rice. Then, I held out my empty hands, surrendering to impermanence.

Finally, I wrote, "I miss you."

"I miss you, too, but the problem—too much need, too much desire. Truth to tell, I wanted friendship, intellectual succor, an ally."

"I did, too," I wrote. "The best part was holding you, but you found someone else for that."

"I know I…"

That was all. A writer who couldn't complete a sentence. The end of his narrative.

Even after a year has passed, he still comes to mind, the way he ran his hand down my side, over my hip, to my thigh.

Near the house are green shoots, corn sprouting from the pollen with which he prayed; now the semblance of what could have been is, and will be.

I bow.

Michael Cadmus

THE BATTLE OF THE FORGOTTEN

I lost the fight as I watched with my arms at my side My freedom is gone away with the definition of me somewhere far behind The mirrors all around shatter in defiance O I lost the fight because I did nothing My mouth moves but there is nothing to hear Sound does not give meaning I don't understand yet neither do they Father John stands at the pulpit screaming for us to ask for forgiveness His hands are covered with blood My body is covered in the same blood of hypocrisy as I kneel and pray My sweat and tears are the sweat and tears of a stone that sees everything, yet is nothing

I. am. nothing.

Michael Cadmus

07501

The face was colorless
The red lips turned pallid
There was no soul
Just a body face up
The eyes closed
No crying could be heard
There was no begging
The name of God
was not called
The maggots had no sympathy
There were no sermons
Only sirens
There was no investigation
Cause it was just another dead body
In a zip code that does not matter

Laura Eklund

IN THE SOUNDS OF A FEATHER

The night will start with a bridge
and end like a tree,
its breath whirring at the water's edge
in the bones of the sea.

The words come without a world
and at rare moments.
He'll dream without a landscape
which could define him.

Love only this feather, this glove,
an enemy or an art
found leaping in an arrow.

In it we are guided with light
and less like time
into the sudden eve of climax,
this fever in a dark-pitched night.

Laura Eklund

HYDRATION AND ASCENSION

The air is unbending
as the peach's leaves turn greener.
In the deep gourds there were pigeons
that flew in high castles
with language we had left.
The river is less as the air breathes
turns green, then greener.
The brain is a chemical refuge,
a place where stars define us
finding the pigeons burned with glass
closing the infertility of time.
We are like a synopsis of straw,
the place where words meet language
and language meets the world.

Ray Keifetz

THE TARTAR

THE TRAIL LED THROUGH A BIRCH WOOD, the sky close, a cold wind blowing up, Mac shouting over the wind.

"You're lucky to be here. "You're lucky..."

As if saying a thing enough times—

"You're lucky, Davey. A foreigner, you can hardly talk. Out here, you don't have to talk. You just do as you're told."

They called him "Davey," his true name too trying for their language.

That name and the life it answered to was just as trying to him, so he kept it to himself, leaving unspoken what could not be. Instead, he thought in pictures—blood, snow, birch trees, and one man, a Tartar, who had tried to save him.

They were roped together for days, he and this Tartar, flesh bleeding, drops falling in a pool at their feet. Roped to each other, and roped in turn to a hard bench, the two men shivered amid a hundred other bound men traveling north in a boarded railroad coach. None of them had wanted to serve in the army. Now, none of them would have to.

The ropes cut deepest whenever the prisoners tried to raise their heads. Chins down, heads bowed, some of them managed, despite the pain, to fall asleep. Their dreams were terrible.

Their screams tore through the car. They cried out to women. Implored. Saints maybe. Maybe whores.

Unlike this Tartar, who was crushing him against the boarded window, Davey could not sleep and, therefore, he did not cry out. To whom would he have cried? What saint, what whore, would hear his prayer? Awake and frozen, he agonized in his silence.

It was always night in the boarded coach. The boards were there to spare the world any glimpse of the prisoners in its midst. Here and there, splinters of light leaked through the cracks, illuminating a swollen jaw, a torn knuckle, the tip of a gash snaking into shadow. Two lanterns at either end of the coach cast just enough light for the Cossack guard to aim his firearm and shoot.

Between swallows of vodka, he walked up and down the narrow central aisle bringing his carbine down on whatever foot stuck out, using the whip to keep himself warm. Each time the Cossack passed the sleeping Tartar, he spat.

The Tartar never stirred and, unlike the other men, never cried out. He slept and slept.

It was said of these Tartars that once they embarked upon journeys of great magnitude, they would not stop until they had reached their destination. It was said that they slept in the saddle, heads nodding to the rhythm of their cantering dreams, trusting their shaggy ponies to carry them through.

This, despite the filthy spittle dripping down his face, was how the Tartar slept now.

For a moment, Davey allowed his own eyes to close, not in the hope of finding sleep, but for the chance to open them, like a Tartar at journey's end, upon a fresh green meadow.

Now, Mac was promising Davey hard bread, dry meat, and sour milk. Taller by a head, and broad, this foreman was stooped.

"Others have come this way. You ain't the first they sent. You work out, or you don't."

DAVEY HARDLY HEARD Mac. He was listening to the one who had been bound to him, who even now still whispered to him—that Tartar who smelt of dung and wind and grass.

Mac stopped, his broad body the size of three Cossack guards blocking the trail. He took a step back, his shoulders snapping off frozen birch branches.

Beyond the birches, the tips of hemlocks scratched at the white sky like fingers.

"What I'm saying, Davey, when you come right down to it, is that there really ain't much to it. There's the herding, the cleaning, the counting, and the killing."

Davey wasn't listening to Mac. He was listening to the whispering of the Tartar—

"Brat—"

The prisoners could cry out to their saints, though they were forbidden to speak with anyone who might answer.

"Brat—"

Davey kept silent.

"Brat, can you understand me?"

Davey glanced down the aisle. The Cossack, his back to them, was almost at the other end of the coach. In a moment, he would reach it, turn—

"Yes."

"Good," the Tartar said, and he started to laugh.

His was a booming horseman's laugh, meant to roll across the steppe, delighting at whatever life brought.

This time it brought a furious Cossack guard. The Cossack struck the laughing Tartar across the forehead with his whip handle. The Tartar crumpled and was still, but the moment the Cossack turned away, the Tartar began to bite at the rope now hidden beneath his slumped body.

"As a sideline," Mac went on, "the trapping 'round here ain't too bad, but you have to stay on top of it. What I mean, Davey, is forget about wolves. You leave a fox, a marten, or even a rabbit for more than a few hours, and half the time all you'll find in your trap is a chewed off paw."

In a frenzy, the Tartar bit at the rope, at his fingers.

Davey leaned over him pretending to sleep.

Each time the guard passed, he spat into both of their faces.

The Tartar seemed to know when to lie still. Davey was surprised that the guard never noticed the biting, that the rest of the prisoners, particularly those roped immediately in front and behind, seemed oblivious to the gnawing and the thrashing. They appeared to be sound asleep. They snored loudly, their dreams for the first time undisturbed by unreachable women.

The prisoners had finally learned to sleep like the Tartar, whose eyes admitted barely enough light for him to see, to consider, to weigh, to plan, to wait—

The Tartar's hand now rested on Davey's knee. A few soaked rope strands still clung to his wrist. He gave Davey a pat, removed his hand, and slowly sat up.

Hands folded primly now in his lap, the Tartar peered around. The absence of a rope had turned him into a passenger, someone free to walk about, have a smoke, and take in the air. He began to whistle a jaunty tune, and then he broke into song.

"Beryezochka, molodovska—"

The Cossack came running. Down slashed the whip. The Tartar raised his left hand and blocked it. He thrust out his right, gripped the Cossack's throat, and twisted. The Cossack sank to his knees; his whip thudded to the floor.

Like a sculptor admiring his handiwork, the Tartar held the dying Cossack at arm's length. Satisfied, he released his grip, and the Cossack pitched face forward onto the floor.

Quickly, the Tartar armed himself, slashed off the ropes that still bound his legs, and then tore into those binding Davey.

The prisoners, suddenly wide awake, raised their bound hands.

The Tartar regarded them thoughtfully for a moment, perhaps wondering what he, a free man, now had in common with any of them. Then, he was among them, loosening their bonds.

Their hands free, the prisoners unbound their legs and began to tear at the boarded windows.

In the cold light, the Tartar donned the Cossack's Astrakhan hat and set the body on his former seat right beside Davey. Fondling the leaded strands of the Cossack's whip, he went to the door and listened.

The train lurched 'round a curve, and the Cossack's body rolled onto Davey, pinning him against the window.

Davey screamed.

The Tartar came running back. He raised the whip and brought it down on the Cossack's lifeless body. Again and again, he flogged the dead man, as if he could not be dead enough.

Panting, the Tartar reached over Davey and wrenched away the planks that covered the window. Peering down at the rushing snow, he said to Davey, "Help me."

The Tartar grabbed the Cossack's body by the armpits and motioned Davey to grab the legs.

"Odin. Dva..."

On each count, they swung the body like a battering ram.

"Tri."

In a cloud of glass, the Cossack's body went flying through the window. Shots rang out. The train braked, throwing everyone to the floor.

Instantly, the prisoners scrambled to their feet. More shots. More shattering glass. Every window disgorging prisoners.

"You first, brat moi."

Davey looked out. Crouched low like animals, the prisoners were running every which way. Bullets struck them, and they fell.

"Jump," the Tartar shouted.

Davey couldn't move.

The Tartar was beating him on the shoulders, lashing him with the Cossack's whip.

"Jump, ladjak. Jump."

At both ends of the coach, the doors swung open. Cossacks rushed in, raised their carbines, and fired.

The Tartar's body slammed into Davey, taking them both through the window.

For ages they fell, clinging to one another, the dying Tartar still begging Davey to jump.

They struck the snow, embracing; at the final darkness, the Tartar's words, "Brat moi, why didn't you——?"

Crossing the Atlantic in the hold of an immigrant ship, Davey carried that word brat—Russian for brother—as he had carried it across Europe, like a locket. He wished he could have separated that consoling word from the remainder of the sentence, but wherever he ran, wherever he hid, the Tartar's last words maintained their grip.

Lying in his bunk below the waterline, he listened to the foreigners, with whom he shared these damp steerage decks, singing their sad songs of the lands they were leaving, the songs and the sea rocking.

If your land was so green and good, why didn't you stay? If my affliction was so desperate, why didn't I jump?

They sang and drank and passed the bottle. The bottle reached him—a sip for a song.

Each time the bottle was passed, he sent it on without drinking. What song could he offer? What melody could he find to accompany his cowardice?

Without a song of his own, he eventually borrowed one. "Beryezochka, molodovska..."

In a grove of young birches, slender and white,
my love is waiting.
In a grove of young birches...

"There's something I've been meaning to ask you," Mac said, when they stopped to rest. It had begun to snow. The few brown leaves still clinging to the branches sighed their last and fluttered aimlessly into the snowflakes. "What's the difference between a Hebrew and a Jew?"

Davey gazed past Mac at the birches. He had never seen trees massed so tightly. A slender man could pass through. "Hebrews," he murmured absently, "the ones in the Bible."

"And the Jews?"

"Jews—" Tasting the strange acrid syllable on his tongue— "the ones they rope to Tartars."

"Aw, you can hardly talk," Mac said. "You call that talking? Say what you mean in plain English. You're not there anymore. You're here."

"Jews, the ones they spit at. The ones they don't let live in their towns. The ones they force into their army—"

"When the king calls, the king calls. King and country is what I say," Mac replied.

"Your king, your country."

"Your king, your country, now," said Mac.

The snow was coming down in wide windy swirls, dissolving the hemlocks into white.

"Let's get a move on," Mac said. "We're almost there."

A sagging wire fence appeared, and a pair of clubs leaning against it. Mac hefted one and handed the other to Davey.

"Let's make this quick," he said and pushed through a break in the wire.

As they continued up the path, Davey could just make out the blurred silhouettes of sheds, lean-tos, and hutches.

"Feed's in that one," Mac pointed. "Over there, whatever tools you'll need. Extra fencing...And that one's yours. That's where you stay."

This shed was not much bigger than the one reserved for picks and shovels.

"Comes with a stove, a bunk. The roof don't leak much. A stove, a bunk, food—what more do you need?"

A roof, a stove, a bunk—shelter, warmth, rest. Was it for these that the prisoners had jumped so eagerly from the train? As they'd raced through the snow, falling over one another in their haste, not one of them had looked back; only the Tartar, his knife slit eyes never fully open in life, as if the light of this world had been unendurable, lay with eyes frozen open, demanding an answer that would let them close again. He had been a nomad, a savage, a man of endless miles. He had ridden across the steppe like a sunbeam, his path straight and piercing. How could he have suspected what Davey now knew to be a fact, that a man could ride all day only to end up where he'd started.

"This is the Pen," Mac said, squinting at the padlocked gate before them. "This is where we go in."

It occurred to Davey, as the foreman fumbled with the icy lock, that he'd been poised to enter this gate his entire life, that his life had been but a series of hasty rehearsals for this moment.

Shivering beyond cold, Davey followed Mac into the Pen. Through the driving snow, he made out a low lean-to hunched like an old man against the wind. Its interior was open to view, but there was nothing to view except darkness.

Davey did as Mac did, and crouched beneath the roof. In the darkness, he heard Mac slide back a wooden door. Gradually, his eyes began to adjust, and he saw a tangle of snouts and bright black eyes shrinking from him.

There must have been hundreds of tiny animals cowering together, a throbbing mound of velvet fur. The creatures cooed and chirped like birds. Above the soft murmuring, another sound, almost human, rose and died.

"They know," Mac whispered. "Somehow, they always do."

Mac began to shiver.

"Tell you what. I'll start up the stove. You get started here. Remember, you don't want to damage the fur." Mac peered down at the tiny animals, then at Davey. "Someone like you. You can hardly talk."

Davey gazed after Mac, watched him close the gate, watched Mac's broad back disappearing into the snow.

Now, Davey was alone in the lean-to. Fingering the club, he paced back and forth, his head scrunched down, as if against a blow.

Through the gloom, he squinted at the facing wall, at the scratches in the rough planks. Slowly, he backed away.

The snow swirled around him, veiling the receding lean-to.

A wisp of smoke reached him, Mac working on the fire.

Now, Davey felt the gate against his back, the gate starting to give—but as if the last strand of blood-soaked rope had finally fallen from his ankles and he was now free to jump or stay, he started back towards the lean-to.

Hefting the club, Davey crouched low and entered. Again the darkness—it was inexhaustible—and in this darkness the murmuring, the twittering, the precious fur—

"Run," he shouted.

They cringed and pressed into each other more tightly, the mass of soft backs rising against the rear wall. Davey raised his club.

Their ears flattened against their heads. They hissed. They spat.

He heard footsteps crunching through the snow behind him. "*Ladjak*," he swore and swung the club at the frozen dirt floor.

"Atta boy, Davey." He heard the foreman's distant shout.

And still, they refused to budge. The stupid, cowardly—yet how lovely they were. Most of them had been born right here in the Pen and knew nothing of the outside world. Confused, frightened, like himself, none of them Tartars.

Boom. He struck the wall inches above their backs.

They flew at him, around him, through his legs, scattering into the snow. Here and there, a few stopped and started scratching at the snow.

Davey smashed the ground behind them, and they shot forward, colliding into Mac just as he reached the Pen.

"The gate, you moron."

Mac brought his own club down. The sound it made. Again and again. "The gate. Shut the gate."

Even with Mac on top of them, one last creature still refused to budge.

Davey grabbed it.

The creature clawed him.

Mac swung.

Davey's shoulder. How it burned. It burned, but he was past Mac and through the gate. The Pen was behind him. He was racing past the sheds. A blast of warm air struck him. A stove, a bunk, food.

From the Pen, Mac called out—

Davey reached the outer fence. He sagged against it. The snow was falling less harshly now. All around him, the woods of this new land, its hemlocks and birches slowly reemerging.

Mac was coming. He was calling, shouting.

The tiny creature in Davey's arms was trembling. Davey stroked it gently.

"Stay where you are." Mac shouted.

"*Brat moi*," Davey whispered and lowered the creature safely to the ground.

Elisavietta Ritchie

THE ANCESTORS WAIT, WET

in the chilly garage
across fields drenched
from days of rain

have waited years in soaked
blue composition books
ink blurred purple or black

inside wooden trunks
keys lost
they persist in manuscripts

schoolboy essays on antique
tsars who tried to transform their lands
outlived their wars or not

written for fathers sisters progeny
for lovers locked in a soggy box
and careless descendants

who could not predict
the height of floods
the rage of hurricanes or wars

John McCarthy

ANATTA

A ghost inside your mouth, my mouth;
      together with no tongue,
we improve the self.

As the self becomes unnecessary,
      the soul emerges.
Thickets of view dissolve.

My life which is your life,
      which is no concept
of we, becomes a part

of the wheel that turns
      then does not turn.
Do not cling to we

or that space between I
      or you; balance,
breathe and repeat.

Eleanor Kedney

BELIEVING IS SEEING

I read in a book an Indian man made it rain.
He knelt beside an ordinary stink bug,
fat-backed and black, poked it with a stick
to make it run and turn, tapped it to flip
until it nearly raised itself on its head;
then thunder rolled, again and again.
What was missing from the story was how
he did it—knowing what to say in a prayer;
believing, then seeing the spirit that moves
in a bug. If only I knew there is more than what I see—
the desert parched, the sky blue for miles;
and that asking for what is needed is an embrace,
first with myself, then with the elements; or how to be
alone with the earth, so she will speak to me.
I don't know what he knew. The *cacti* are dying
and *javelinas* are in the backyard searching
for water, and I put my hands together,
ask for a hard rain.

Ruth Ann Dandrea

THE CAT AND THE INDIAN WOMAN

THE CAT WAS small, almost equally white and black, and though feral, clean and soft-looking.

The Indian woman was also small. She wore colorful clothes of deep yellows, important reds, oranges and sapphires, and was completely tame.

There was nothing extraordinary about the cat. Everything about the Indian woman was extraordinary.

The cat appeared on the porch, mewling one morning at the door, the door which the Indian woman rarely closed and never locked. It's possible that the cat had slept inside on the landing or the steps on any number of nights, unnoticed. It's possible, as unconcerned as the Indian woman could be, that the cat had a passel of kittens hidden in one of the multitudinous clay pots the Indian woman left in the stairwell.

I didn't mind the cat.

I didn't mind the Indian woman, either.

She was one of the only people I didn't mind.

I watched from my window, as she came and went. Her step on the stairs was soft and slow, silent almost as a cat's.

From her upstairs apartment emanated sometimes some sort of stringed Hindi instrument, sometimes an *om shantih* chanting. Sometimes the scent of incense, sweet and bitter at the same time, came seeping through the ceiling.

At first, it scared me some, but I grew to accept it. I grew to expect it and expected it enough to need it.

She was small and dark, moving like a shadow over the porch past my window to water the begonia in the bucket by the porch rail.

The cat was small enough to curl into a sleep circle on the railing above the begonia, so as to greet the Indian woman eye-to-eye, when she stooped to water the flower.

The cat never missed a watering.

The Indian woman kept no schedule that I could discern. I wondered how the cat knew, but I knew it did know and that it negotiated its naps to be able to lift its round ball head and perk its ears, alert as if clipped with pinking shears, to unveil fairy-thin eyelids, exposing to the light the amber-green eyes, at just the moment the Indian woman's gaze would graze its body, ruffling its fur like a passing zephyr.

The Indian woman never touched the cat.

Her behavior toward it shifted, though—from an insistent scooting on the first meeting to a gentle shooing on the second or third or fourth, to a noncommittal acceptance of the creature's inhabitance of her porch, to once, with haphazard detachment, the placing on the stoop of a saucer of milk, which the cat lapped daintily, tiny petal tongue descending into the creamy lake, disappearing into the impossible mouth.

After that, I saw the cat sidle itself against the Indian woman's leg. The cat made her grateful trek across the flat of the porch, before the Indian woman reached the second set of stairs, before her plump hands gripped the iron rail to aid her feet in their slow descent; or after they released the rail to rest, before she began the harder, longer climb of the inside stairs.

The cat, appeared a ghost motion, eased its furred flank just once, not winding in and out, cautious perhaps of the scat of hand or of tangling itself in her *sari*, against the leg which felt—what?— maybe the momentary heat of its passing presence?

The Indian woman removed herself to Bangalore in winter.

She returned when the first flowers bloomed.

The end of the cold season brought daffodils and croci, but her footsteps didn't tread the wooden porch boards until lupine luxuriated purple-y up sturdy stems; when poppies opened red-lipped, black-tongued mouths; and daisies lifted yellow eyes to a dependable sun.

I don't know how the cat weathered snow and ice. I don't know where it fed and slept. Maybe it visited some Bosnian woman across town, a Karen émigré with a warm kitchen, or slept itself under the kitchen of a Thai restaurant, dreaming in curry.

On the day that the bright bundle of Indian woman re-appeared on the porch, the cat did, too. The cat remembered and returned.

Waiting for breath to return, after the third step, the Indian woman spoke to the cat. "Are you still here, then, old friend?"

A tilt of furred head, a twitch of triangular ear, a listening stance.

"We made it through another winter, you and me." The sentence began with the uptilt tone of a question, but ended a stolid statement. Truth. Visible and real. The two creatures, woman and cat, attached by the rub of fur in Utica sunshine.

They wouldn't make it through another winter, though.

Not even a summer.

Just days later, the Indian woman would be asleep on a stoop, surrounded by flowers, the cat keeping vigil.

Both would vanish then, and other feet, many of them, would pound the stairwell to her rooms; would tromp the porch, forgetting the begonia flower; would carry in and carry out boxes and crates, bouquets and trays of sweet smelling treats.

Everyone knew the Indian woman.

No one knew the cat but me. I knew it by the chant she sang the night before she died.

The high thin appeal of her voice leaked through the floorboards. A deep, low, opposite timbre, its own harmony:

om jayanti mangala kali bhadrakali kapalini.
durga ksama siva dhatri svaha svadha namostute

Calling Kali.

Begging the goddess of death, whose name means "time," whose name means "time has come," who waves her scimitar to annihilate evil. Ultimate reality is her other name.

Books will tell you she rides a lion, but like life, the lion is a shape-shifter.

Sometimes, it looks like a small black-and-white cat.

Sometimes, a small, furred creature, lithe and pure, is all that is needed to ease a peaceful soul.

The cat disappeared the day the Indian woman died.

But she isn't gone.

Rich Campbell

OSSUARY

Why pretend it is only a dream,
this dark wish,
to build a beauty-white bone church
on the west edge of today
midst bitter and contorted oaks?

There we could ponder,
from high-back alabaster *cathedra*,
the rattle bone homilies
of our tomorrows.

Or sing melodic dirges
on vivid-dark days
to heads without ears,
and mouths with no tongues.

And why not go there,
when sun beams
through slats of rib-vaulted nave,
to waltz, triple-time,
our (once) beautiful dead?

Rich Campbell

MEDICINE BUNDLES

Somewhere near the center,
the student paper I read tonight said:
"I really have found it
kind of creepy that some of the
Indians
would make a little doll
of the hair of their dead loved one
and carry it with them
(in their medicine bundle)."

First, I thought of my brother's ashes
(waiting, enclosed these years)
on my bookshelf by the bed,
in a box labeled Brahman Mortuary.

And then, I wondered if I
shouldn't maybe
be carrying part of him with me,
in my vest pocket? Or should I be

sifting him into the Cedar River?
Sending him with this Fall's winds?

And would it matter so much either,
or any, way?

After a long minute, I entered a ten in the grade book.
I wrote "good job" on the paper.

What else should I have said that she might carry with her?
And anyway I was wondering about my brother, now.

Khanh Ha

THE GENERAL IS SLEEPING

SHE WAS RAIL THIN and tall. After three days lying in the same hospital bed, I could tell upon waking that she had been in the room, while I was sleeping. An unmistakable musk in the air came from her body. A fragrance perhaps.

Coming out of sedation for the first time, I had felt clean below. Someone must have washed me.

I was clad only in a hospital gown. My right leg was suspended in a contraption, a pulley and a horizontal metal rod overhead. The leg seemed to have a life of its own, after having been crushed in a head-on collision between my car and a drunk driver's.

On the second day when the pain became bad, they gave me medication for it. I woke, feeling as if the pillow were a giant beanbag, feeling very cool between the legs from a moist antiseptic tissue.

The rubbing. I decided to be asleep while I was being cleaned there. I heard the rustle of a gown and then felt the warmth of a washcloth pressed against my face. I smelled her musk scent.

I opened my eyes.

A golden-brown face was looking down at me. The long-lashed eyes gleamed. The smile revealed dazzlingly white teeth.

"Ah, you're awake now." Holding the washcloth, she watched me.

I said a hello, but I couldn't hear the word I spoke for the drumming in my head. I felt drugged.

She stooped to look me full in the face. "How are you this evening, Mr. Lee?" She spoke with an accent.

"Leh," I said. "Not Lee." I spelled it for her.

"Ah, Mr. Leigh. I'm Aida."

I was amused by how she pronounced my last name, the small tongue roll with the L.

She dabbed my stitched forehead with the washcloth. The musky aroma went with her hand. Her oval face was delicate. She was in her twenties, perhaps. Her cornrows were knotted into a thick plait, slung over her shoulder onto her chest.

"I'll bring your dinner, Mr. Leigh." She straightened.

Tall. Very tall in her blue uniform. If I were to stand next to her, my head would be to her ears.

"Where are you from?" I asked, squinting.

"I'm from Senegal."

"Do you speak French?"

"Yes. Do you, Mr. Leigh?"

"A little. My father spoke French fluently."

"Ah. It brightens my day whenever I hear someone speak French." Her clear voice had a resonance. Then, frowning, she leaned her head to one side. "You have received no visitors since you're here?"

"My father died some years ago."

"What about your mother, Mr. Leigh?"

"She died shortly after my father's death, and I have no siblings."

Aida folded the washcloth. "Are you married, Mr. Leigh?"

"I was once."

"Did she know about your accident?"

"No. And even if she did..."

My voice was curt, and Aida dipped her head. "You sound like you have something against her?"

"She hated my family," I blurted out.

"How come?"

"In fact, she hated my father."

"Why?"

My chest heaved. "My father and my mother did not attend our wedding. It embarrassed me, but it humiliated my wife. My ex-wife. If there's one person in this world she hated most, it's my father."

"I don't assume that your father was a terrible man."

"Thank you." I nodded at her gentle smile. I still felt self-conscious that she was the one who had been cleaning my body.

"So what happened?"

"My wife—my ex-wife—had never told me about her own family, though she knew much about mine. When we decided to get married, she told me about her father. He used to be a celebrated musician in South Vietnam. Millions of fans idolized him. To me, he was a gentleman, and I liked him. Then, I brought the news of our engagement home to my father, and hell broke out."

Aida blinked. She had dense lashes with a dramatic upsweep. Her longish eyes were God-made beauty.

"My father told me, 'That scumbag is a Communist. He lives right in our backyard, and we can't do nothing about it.' I said, 'How do you know?' and he said, 'He's a mole. We have many moles and termites like him in our army, too. We executed several of them, but we couldn't touch a man of his stature.'"

"This was back in Vietnam during the war, Mr. Leigh? You and she..."

"No, after we came to America. We met here, but our past never died. I mean her father's past."

"And what did your father do during the war?"

"My father was a general, a four-star general of the Army of the Republic of Vietnam."

"Ah. So he was a big shot." She squinted her eyes. "It must have been very difficult for him to leave Vietnam and come here."

"It was."

"For a man of his position, I'm sure." She put the washcloth into her blouse pocket. "What did he do in this country, Mr. Leigh?"

"He drove a forklift." I paused. "From five to midnight. Every night."

"I guess nobody around your father knew who that forklift operator really was." She smiled with a slight nod. "Yes?"

"Yes, just an old Asian man who came to work every night with a dinner box his wife packed for him. Every night for nine years."

"Then what, Mr. Leigh?"

"Then his kidneys started failing. He had diabetes. Eventually," I kept nodding to the unfinished sentence, "he lost a leg to amputation, and from there he went downhill fast."

We both glanced at my leg in the stirrup.

Aida went around the bed to the other side to check on the urinary catheter. "You need to drink more," she said, dropping my gown down. "You still think a lot about your ex-wife, yes?"

I held her gaze, until she blinked. Those almond-shaped eyes made my heart go soft. "Yes," I said.

"What about her?"

I tried to smile.

It must have looked like a grimace to her, for she took my hand in hers, held it, and said, "You have nice hands, Mr. Leigh. Like my people's."

She opened her hand, the fingers long and tapered with symmetrical nails. "Let me get your dinner. Are you hungry, Mr. Leigh?"

My HANDS SHOOK, so she fed me.

I didn't have a brain injury, but besides the gash on my forehead and my shattered shinbone, I must have had a mild concussion. At least I knew that much after a series of tests. This explained why my hands trembled, when I tried to feed myself.

I wasn't feeling hungry, only numb in my lower leg. In time, the dullness would give way to pangs that my brain remembered well.

Aida placed the tray on its legs over my lap; the food smelled warm, unappetizing.

"Do you like lentil soup, Mr. Leigh?" she asked, as she lowered the bed and sat down on a chair.

"I like clam chowder."

"I'll check with the kitchen the next time."

She spoon-fed me.

My tongue felt like rubber, and not until the bowl was near empty did I begin to register an aftertaste of lentil. I watched her slicing through the golden breaded chicken cutlet.

"I knew this man," I said to her, "a male nurse who took care of my father, when he was confined to a nursing home."

Aida fed me a piece of chicken, her lips slightly parted, as I opened my mouth.

"He was like you, a Senegalese."

"Really." She spooned some mashed potato, and I ate that. Then, she pierced a baby carrot with the fork and held it until I opened my mouth again. "What's his name?"

"Ibou." I chewed the soft baby carrot. I liked carrots, and their familiar smell suddenly made me feel homesick.

She fed me another slice of chicken. "Was he also young like me?"

"No. He was a senior nurse." I swallowed and sighed. "He loved to speak French with my father."

"*C'est beau.*"

"He found out that my father was once a four-star general, that he was a Viet Minh who fought the French during the Indochina War. Ibou told my father that his own father was with the French Foreign Legion that fought in Dien Bien Phu in 1954, a decorated soldier who lost a leg during the siege. Ibou joked with my father—Wouldn't it be extraordinary if it was my father who had set the trap that claimed his father's leg?"

Aida's lips parted. Then, she smiled.

She had a perfectly shaped upper lip; her full lower lip pouted, when she did not smile.

"You two must be of the same age, yes?" she said.

"I'm thirty-six. I couldn't tell exactly how old he was."

"We Senegalese do look younger than we are, just like the Asians." She tilted her head, as if to avoid my gaze. "Did he make an impression on you?"

"He was always polite. I remember his accent—like yours. He was some kind of a rare species."

Her eyes opened wide, lips puckered. "How do you mean, Mr. Leigh?"

"He must have been at least seven feet tall." I looked toward the door and back at her. "Whenever he entered the room, he had to lower his head. Have you seen anyone like that back home?"

"Tall men? Yes, but not that tall." She offered me a gulp of chocolate milk, and I gladly obliged, for she'd told me that I ought to drink more. "Did you get along with him like your father did?"

"Yes. Ibou was a gentleman."

She was about to feed me another slice of chicken, but I held up a hand. "I'm full."

She peeled the lid off of a cup of red Jell-O.

While its raspberry flavor burst in my mouth, she pinched a fleck of gelatin off of my lips. Her musky fragrance mixed with the raspberry.

"So he took care of your father," she said. "For how long?"

"Two years. Until my father died." I dropped my gaze to her hand. "He used to change my father's clothes all by himself. Before Ibou, it took two female nurses to do that chore. My father's imbalance after losing the leg made it harder to change him out of his clothes or to dress him, but Ibou did those things so effortlessly that he became my father's sole caretaker."

"You were married then?" She paused with the spoon in midair.

"Yes, but my wife never visited my father."

"Your ex-wife must be beautiful, yes?"

"To me."

"And you must have had lots of girls before you met her?" As she brought the spoon to my mouth, her little finger touched my lips. At my smile, she tipped her head back. "Short girls, tall girls. Americans, Asians. Yes?"

I chuckled, shaking my head.

She said, "How tall are you, Mr. Leigh?"

"Five-seven." I nodded at her. "And you?"

"Five-eleven."

"You don't need high heels, ever."

"I don't look right in them, I'm sure."

"You're long-legged, like those *Vogue* girls, except they're on spike heels."

"Those million-dollar girls." Aida shook her head, her eyes trailing away. "I don't look anything like them."

"No, you don't." I saw a startled look in her eyes. "You look plain and beautiful—the way you are."

Her eyes flinched, then became soft. I thought I saw a blush on her cheeks, for the first time.

"I used to be self-conscious about my skin," she said, "because my mother told me how life was, when she grew up in the colonial time. Black skin was despised, forbidden to mix with white society without permission. Growing up, my mother was an educated and beautiful girl, and yet she dreaded the color of own skin so much that she wanted to cover her arms and neck, to put on a big straw hat with a veil to hide her face. Age gave her maturity. She did not want me to suffer the same identity crisis, though she still feared that someday I might have *mulatto* children. She took me to social events, where I performed our *sabar* dance, to express myself in the free form of footwork and arm movements. She made me aware of such words as *nègres* and *négresses*, telling me that the word *noir* for black had ceased to exist after the 1791 massacres in Santo Domingo."

Aida paused. Her large, gleaming eyes held me with a gentle smile. "Do you know about the Santo Domingo massacres?"

"No," I said, feeling ignorant.

She went on to give me a brief history of the slave revolt in the French colony of Santo Domingo that led to the expulsion of the French colonial government, and hence the establishment of the independent Republic of Haiti.

She put down the empty Jell-O cup and smiled. "Here," she said, picking up one of the two cookies. "I threw these in. They only give you one kind of dessert."

"Jell-O and cookies." I took a small bite of one cookie and then picked up the other for her. "Please. Try it, if you like. Cinnamon cookie."

She nibbled at it. I watched her drooping eyelids. Those thick lashes with their beautiful curl didn't need mascara.

She looked up. "What do you do, Mr. Leigh?"

"Call me Minh."

"Min?" She made a humming sound with the M.

I reached for the glass of milk. "I'm a photographer."

"So you take pictures? Of what?" She looked at me with a spark in her eyes.

"I shoot advertising photography, for print catalogs. Things that you browse before you decide to buy."

"Not fashion photography?" she said with a trailing smile.

"Just an old-fashioned photography business. No fashion models or nude girls."

Her fluty laugh sounded girlish. She tossed her head back, and her hair plait swung behind the nape of her neck. For the first time I noticed her elegant and slender neck, framed by the round neckline.

"Were you close to your father, Mr. Leigh?"

"Minh." I put the last piece of cookie into my mouth. "I was not."

"Ah. But you love him, don't you, Min?"

I said nothing. Then, I nodded. "It took me all my life to feel that—after he died."

"In his condition, he must have looked to you for care." She tore open the packet of sanitizer and gave me one wet tissue. "I'm very close to my mother. She almost died giving birth to me, but God saved her and me," she said.

"Where is she now?"

"Back home. With my father." Aida covered the meal plate with its lid. "My father was struck with a viral disease, once. He bled in his bowels and in his nose, and there was blood in his urine. Hemorrhagic fever. We were with him all the time during his illness, because he needed us. He cried when he was alone, for it made him think death was waiting for that rare moment to take him away in his sleep."

I cleaned my mouth with the wet wipe. I couldn't help remembering the sanitizing smell that hung in the room, whenever she cleaned my body as I slept. "My father was different," I said to her. "He really was."

"He didn't need you? I mean, we all need love and care." Slowly, she folded my tissue into quarters. "Maybe he didn't want to show you his tender side, yes?"

"To the best of my recollection, I can't say that he was an affectionate father. Maybe I was insensitive to what he might've needed from me."

No, I never felt close to my father.

I told Aida about incidents during my boyhood, how when I did something terribly wrong, he would lash me. To keep count, he had our chauffeur, a corporal, call out each lash. One. Two. Three. Four. To this day, I still heard the counting.

I had thought of him often after the car accident. Now, I thought of him, while the doctor made a thorough evaluation of my shattered leg, while an orderly wheeled me back to my room.

Could my leg be saved? The doctor would tell me soon.

It was evening. I had not eaten dinner.

Through the window I could see a full moon. I didn't feel pain in the leg, at least for now. I wouldn't until the pain killer wore off.

Closing my eyes to rest, I smelled the familiar musk in the room. She must have been here, while I was taken to the examination room.

A female nurse brought in my dinner tray.

"Can you eat by yourself?" she said, as she placed the tray over my lap.

"Sure." I pushed the control to raise the adjustable head section.

"If you need anything else, please ring." She glanced at my leg suspended in midair. "You have any pain, Mr. Lee?"

"Not at this moment." I slid up on the bed. "Where's Aida?"

"She's on her rounds. We have a new patient."

I ate only after the nurse left. My hands still shook, so I concentrated on each movement.

I sipped some apple juice, looking at the tray. It held baked salmon, mashed potatoes, peas, and carrots. There was also a bowl of chicken noodle soup and a slice of chocolate cake for dessert.

I took a deep breath. Sometime tonight, the doctor would come in and tell me the news.

My father had looked calm on the day he'd had his leg amputated above the knee. If I hadn't lifted his gown to look at what then resembled a stump, I would have sworn it was any other day to him. He didn't mention the surgery that day, though he asked me the next time to come in with my mother.

"Do not let her drive," he said. "Her nerves are very fragile, now."

Later Ibou told me something that has haunted me since. "The general did not remember," Ibou said, always referring to my father by that title. "This is common, after you wake up from a surgery. When I changed him, he pulled up his legs, and trust me, Mr. Leh, a thousand words could not describe that look in his eyes. The general recovered quickly, though. I don't mean his physical recovery. A moment later, the general began to chat with me in French.

"Oh-la-la." Ibou laughed heartily. "He told me things."

"What things?" I asked.

Ibou said, "Fragments of his life as a boy and as a soldier. Fascinating. One day I asked him if he could read them into a cassette for me, and he said, '*Bien sûr, mon ami.*'

"So I brought in a mini-cassette recorder, and during his undisturbed moments he spoke those stories into the recorder. When he gave me the whole thing back, he asked me, '*Pourquoi voulez-vous de garder ces histoires?*'

"I told him, 'General, I'm a writer.'

"'*Un écrivain?*' he said. '*C'est très noble.*'

"One story I couldn't shake off took place in the summer of 1972. He called that summer the Blazing Summer. The Vietnam War was at its worst.

That summer, the Vietnamese marines recaptured Quang Tri Province. From Hue, a convoy was dispatched to Quang Tri to relieve the marines and to reinstall the former administration. Escorted back to the city were the exiled province chief and his entourage. Local merchants and residents tagged along behind the convoy, to return home. The general was one of them."

Ibou shook a finger as if to warn me not to ask questions.

I did not.

He continued. "The convoy had to cross a bridge. Just as it approached the bridgehead, shelling exploded. From a nearby mountain the Viet Cong was firing mortars. The mile-long convoy was broken up. After many rounds of shelling, the Viet Cong failed to hit the bridge.

"Suddenly, all eyes fell upon an old woman who appeared out of nowhere. She was carrying two cane baskets suspended from a shoulder pole. In one was her clothing, in the other a little boy. The shelling had trapped her in the middle of the bridge. She froze.

"No one from the convoy dared leave his cover, but the general jumped up and raced toward her. He carried the boy and half-carried the old woman back to the roadside shelter.

"Within minutes, air support came. Soon, the convoy got rolling again."

Ibou put his hand on my shoulder. "Now, you may ask why the general disguised himself as a commoner. *Très bien.* He disguised himself, so he could assess the morale of the troops and the civilians, and to take in first-hand the damages to the city against possible false reports."

I TOLD AIDA the story.

When she entered the room, I was resting, half-reclined with the dinner tray on my lap, the meal unfinished, my eyes closed. The musk scent woke me from my reflection.

I noticed the cardinal-red ribbon that adorned her usually plain plait. I couldn't help saying, "It looks pretty on you, Aida."

"Thank you, Min," she said, looking down at me and then at my dinner.

"Where were you?" I already knew the answer, but I still wanted to hear it from her.

"I was in here earlier. You were being examined, so I went to where they needed me." She touched the cup of chicken noodle soup, still lidded. "It's getting warm. Do you want me to reheat it, Min?"

"Don't bother. Do you have to go soon?"

"No, I'm on my break." Glancing at the meal, she said, "Let me see if you can eat by yourself."

I removed the lid of the soup cup, while she watched. I was distracted by the musk scent, and my hand started trembling.

She deftly pressed the control button, so that the bed dropped, whirring. She sat down on the chair and took the cup from my hand.

"You're on your break, Aida," I said meekly.

"That's why I'm here." She held her smile as she brought the spoon to my lips.

Taking her time between spoonfuls, she asked me about the examination.

I told her that within an hour or two I would know.

"Know what they will do with your leg?" she said casting a glance at my suspended leg.

Sighing, I nodded.

"You didn't want to eat. You must be worried, yes?"

"I'm fine." I lied.

"You should pray, Min. It will take the worries and fears off your mind."

"I don't see how." My throat felt dry despite the soup. "I never believed in prayer."

"My father said that it's belief, faith that keeps men in touch with the supernatural beyond the praying and the worshiping. He said men are ignorant enough to think they can get along by themselves and that nothing they can't see or own matters." She put the cup down, took my hand, and held it between hers. "Just open your mind and pray, Min."

I bit my lips at the earnest look in her eyes and nodded like a simpleton.

My father had derided priests and monks. When my mother asked him, during a moment of his lucidity, if she could have a religious rite for his funeral, my father smirked. "Them priests and monks," he said. "Their spiritual lives are nothing but the empty sounds of recitation and chanting. Without a pagoda, without a church, what'd become of their spiritual lives? Eh?"

I couldn't say whether or not he had sowed that notion of distrust in my mind.

Aida looked lost in thought. Then, she said, "Min, I'll pray for you, so you won't end up like your father. You never asked him much about his life, no?"

"No, I'd never asked him anything. Maybe someday I'd read somebody else's stories about him. That's my dad, I'd say."

"And Ibou would be the author?"

We both laughed. Aida canted her head to look at me. "Who do you look like? Your mother or your father?"

"My mother. I have no resemblance to my father."

"You sound like you deny it," she said, smiling.

I gazed her lips, and she blushed.

"In her younger days," I said, "my mother had the kind of beauty that you'd call classic. I wonder what made her fall in love with my father." I cut the chocolate cake in half, lifted a piece with a napkin, and pushed the other piece on the plate toward her. "Please, share it with me."

She forked a piece, and I noticed that she was left-handed. "Your father must've adored your mother," she said, taking a bite.

"He was unfaithful to her," I said, before I'd thought it through. "She told me so, after he'd become an invalid. I guess she'd bottled it up all her life.

"She must have been upset with the way he perked up when he was with Ibou, becoming suddenly animated and carrying on and on in their small talks, in French, of course.

"When she was with him, he'd clam up. Most patients, I noticed, couldn't wait to see their loved ones. It's dreary and downright lonesome for most of them, but he didn't need her, his wife."

Aida sat riveted, nibbling her lower lip. "How did he...betray her?"

"Women have uncanny instincts. Don't you agree?" I asked.

Her eyes glinted with amusement, as she nodded.

"I didn't ask my mother what triggered her suspicion, but at one point she told our chauffeur, the corporal, to report to her every place he drove my father. You see, my mother was the godmother of our chauffeur's little daughter, so he was loyal to her.

"He told her that every day around noon he dropped my father off in downtown Saigon, where he'd spend an hour or two in a pharmacy.

"One day, after dropping my father off at the usual place, our chauffeur came back and drove my mother to that place.

"My mother waited in the car, while it was parked outside the pharmacy, until my father came out.

"When he got into the car, her presence shocked the daylight out of him.

"She asked him to wait. Then, she went into the pharmacy. Fifteen minutes later she came back out, got into the car, and told the chauffeur to drive home.

"From that day on, my father quit going to visit his mistress."

"His mistress?" Aida's eyes widened.

"You wonder how my mother found out? She happened to go through his wallet one day and saw a picture of a woman. Yes, someone else's photo besides hers in his wallet. How foolish of him to keep his woman's picture, but I guess we're all blind when we're in love, aren't we?" I shook my head.

Aida chuckled. Her eyes looked dreamy. "It must've shocked your mother deeply when she saw the photograph of your father's mistress. I would be shocked too, if something of that nature happened to me."

"It tore her to pieces. She could never have imagined such a horrible thing. A man of his stature? A man who was so madly in love with her when they first met that he kept count of the days being away from her by marking a cut with a nail on his rifle's buttstock?

"You know what my mother did when she came upon the woman's picture?"

I met Aida's eyes. She hadn't touched the rest of her cake.

"She cut it up and left the pieces in his wallet, this picture of his courtesan."

Aida giggled. "I like that word."

"That's the word my mother used, when she told me the story. I thought she used this word, because my father was a man of rank, like a king at that time."

"Do you have any love for him, Min?"

"I've thought of him a lot, since he died. My father is a good man."

"Of course."

"He never impressed me as a loving father, but he had a heart of gold. I knew this from an incident."

"Another incident? Back home?"

"No, here." I offered her my glass of apple juice, and she took it. "I was working at this advertising agency—my first job out of college. One late afternoon, just before I left my cubicle, I saw an Asian woman, a janitor. She was in her fifties. She must've been in earlier than usual, because I'd never seen her before. She was dusting each cubicle, probably waiting for everyone to leave, before vacuuming the floor. She didn't make a sound.

"When she reached my cubicle, I sensed her standing behind my chair. I decided to keep busy. When I finally turned around, she was still standing there. She gestured with her duster toward a framed picture on my desk.

"'Is that your father?' she asked in plain Vietnamese.

"I said, 'Yes.'

"In that picture, I was about five years old, sitting between my mother and my father.

"The cleaning woman took a step closer to my desk and said, 'He was in jail in 1961, right, Mister?'

"Something knifed my gut. I nodded. He had been in the prison of what used to be the Lê Lei artillery barracks, after the military *coup d'etat* which had been carried out to overthrow President Diem, failed. My father, then a major general, was sentenced to life. That much I knew from my mother.

"The woman's gaze never left the framed picture on my desk, and I grew irritated.

"'Thank Heaven and the Buddha,' she blurted. 'I knew it was him. I looked at his picture every night, when I came in to clean, but I didn't know who to ask about it. Mister, I don't have many debts in my life but one. A debt I owe your father for the welfare of my family, and...'

"She stuttered. For a moment she looked like a jabbering mental patient. 'It had to do with my son...'

"'Your son?' I said to her. 'Where is he now?'

"'He's studying to become a doctor now, in California. This debt had to do with my son, when he was a few months old. In 1961, I was put into jail in Saigon by the government.'

"I looked at her, no longer irritated but intrigued. 'What did you do to be thrown in jail?'

"'They charged me with conspiracy of silence,' she said. 'It happened after my husband suddenly disappeared. I didn't know where he went, but I knew he was taken by the Viet Cong. This happened all the time in my village. The Viet Cong said they recruited you, but nobody could ever say no to them. I reported his disappearance to the local authorities. They questioned me and asked me to come back in a week. I came back the next week.

"'Where's your husband? Back yet?' they asked.

"'No,' he's still gone, 'I told them.' That's when they arrested me.

"They said, 'We know where he went. Tell us where to find his base.'

"I couldn't tell them anything. How could I?

"They drove me and my four-month old baby to Saigon and put us into the police headquarters' jail. In that courtyard, they took us to Ward B. That was the ward for Viet Cong. We were kept in Cell Number One, the only cell for females.'

"I kept my gaze on her, as she went on.

"'I was tortured every day. They forced me to drink soapy water 'til I became bloated. Then, someone stepped on my stomach, and water came out of my mouth and my nose. The next day they jammed wires under my fingernails and turned on the current. My whole body jumped and went numb. I thought I'd lost all my limbs.

"'By the third day, my baby got sick. They had given us no blankets, though everyone else had them. It could be hot outside, but it was chilly inside—all the time. You know, Mister, there in those damp cells, a blanket equals life. Without one, prisoners often caught pneumonia and died before receiving medical attention.'

"I stared at her. My body tensed up.

"She continued. 'My baby began having diarrhea. His cries kept everyone in the other cells awake at night. By the end of the first week, he'd lost so much body fluid that he became unconscious. I couldn't breast-feed him, anymore. I cradled him with what was left of me to keep him warm, but he was going away.

"'Someone from another cell gave up his own blanket for my baby. When they passed down the blanket, they said it was from Anh Ba—Brother Number Three. I heard that from that night on, he slept on the floor with a rush mat wrapped around him to keep warm. His blanket brought my baby back to life. The diarrhea stopped, and he was feeding again.

"'One month later, I was freed. When the warden let us out, I turned left instead of right for the exit.

"'You want to stay, woman?' the warden said.

"'No, sir, I said, but allow me to thank Anh Ba.'

"I went up to his cell. Cell Number Four, I remember to this day. There were three men in that cell. Anh Ba was a man in his early thirties. I put my baby down, prostrated myself in front of his cell, and kowtowed to him three times.

"He waved me off, obviously embarrassed.

"I said to him, Ân *nhân*—savior—my son and I will owe you this debt for the rest of our lives. I have nothing to give you in return, so please accept my three kowtows as my gratitude to you. I wept in the silence of Ward B, as people in the other cells listened. Then, I got up, bowed to him, and left.'"

This was the janitor's story.

Aida handed me the glass of apple juice. "Your father is an unusual man," she said, with a note of admiration in her voice.

I nodded in agreement. One of the reasons I had talked at length with her was that she knew how to listen. Then, there was something called compatibility. I had thought about that, after my mother told me of my father's infidelity. Perhaps he found not only compatibility but also the fire that lit up his soul in his courtesan.

Entering the room was the nurse who'd brought my dinner. Aida said to her, "He's almost done. Let me take care of this."

"Sure," the nurse said. "Also, Doctor River will be here in half an hour to discuss the medical issue with Mr. Lee."

"Half an hour?" Aida and I looked at the wall clock. It was 9:30p.m.

After the nurse left, Aida sat with her eyes on the floor. When she finally looked up, I saw a grim expression on her face. "Are you afraid, Min?"

"Perhaps," I said. In fact, I felt calm. Remembering my father and his indifferent attitude toward his own physical tragedy had given me the much needed mettle.

"I'll be back at ten." Aida rose, lifting the tray from the bed. Her eyes, beautiful in their brooding, blinked, as she bent and kissed me on the forehead.

"I'll go and pray for you."

SHE DIMMED THE LIGHT, as she left.

I listened to the wall clock tick, as I lay looking at the ceiling. The leg didn't hurt, save the occasional throbbing.

What did Doctor River see, after he'd run the battery of tests earlier in the evening?

I wasn't there on the day the doctor told my mother and my father that—against the threat of gangrene—they had to amputate his right leg. The amputation, they always said, is to take a step toward improving the quality of your life.

When my mother and I visited him later in the nursing home, my father never talked about his handicap. If I mentioned his amputation, his answers were casual, as if he were talking about a missing slipper. When my mother and I left at the end of our visit, there was no gloominess about him. Sometimes, looking back toward him, I would see him turn his face toward the window and sleep.

What did he think of while he was awake, with all the time he had, lying in bed or being wheeled outside for fresh air? I often wondered. Time must be painfully slow to pass for him, but then I wasn't him. I never had his mettle, his absence of self-pity.

One day, when I came into his room, he simply looked at me and smiled.

My mother said, "That's Minh."

He kept smiling, as if he and I never met. Only the sight of Ibou still stirred him up with excitement and brought back slivers of his memory.

After he died in the hospital, Ibou called me, asking how the general was doing. I told him.

I was in the hospital room, where my father lay with a white sheet covering his body, when Ibou came in.

He stood by the bed, looking down at my father for some time, then crossed himself.

"The general is sleeping," he said.

NOW, I HEARD VOICES in the hallway. I could hear Doctor River's voice. I closed my eyes. They were still talking outside.

Then I smelled musk. She was here.

Lyn Lifshin

BLACK RAIN, HIROSHIMA

i.

It was as if we
were thrown into
a smelting furnace.
My friend had skin
hanging down like
the meltings of a
candle. Many ran
to the cool of any
water they could
find, hurled them
selves into sewers
or headed for the
River Ota that
soon was thick with
the dead and dying.
Some died on the
river bank, their
heads in the water,
having used their
last surge of earthly
energy for a drink

ii.

Hiromu Morishiti found
her father later that
day lying in a grassy
field. He'd been on

a street car near
downtown, on his
way to work. She
cremated him in
her garden that
night, his eyes
like those of grilled
fish. Others slept on
Hijiama Hill, looked
down on the place that
once was their city,
lay calling for
mothers, calling
for children, calling
for water then not
calling at all

William Varner

COUNTY

*This correspondence is forwarded from the York County Jail. The contents have
not been evaluated. The York County Jail is not responsible for the substance
of content of the closed communications.*

—Stamped on Every Envelope

Rain on the window, rain on the razor wire
    early a.m. the fluorescent lights flutter to life
the cell doors unlock down the rows
    like tongues clucking in quarter notes
cheap yellow disposable razors
    a palmful of white Barbasol foam, the shower
scalding hot this time of day, everyone gathered
    around the TV watching the morning news and weather
    as if it mattered
the latest mug shots from the local towns displayed
    and judged, laughter at another criminal's stupidity
    or perversion
meals come with a plastic spork
oatmeal, stale bread and dry muffins
    pinto beans, refried beans, nameless pale beans
    with a smattering
of dead maggots, bologna the color of a light bruise,
    no condiments, no salt and pepper
the only thing to eat sweet apples and unripe oranges
    detoxing addicts and alcoholics dropping their trays,
    hands shaking
unable to clean up the mess, all of us laughing
    back into, back out of, back into, back out of our cells
no sleeping under blankets during the day
others bring a mop and cleaning supplies to keep the stainless
    steel toilet shining

almost every day brings a new cellmate
domestic assault, a fifth OUI
    the skinner who smells like fresh cat litter running in
    place for exercise
one paranoid schizophrenic kid so crazy he hallucinates
    severed heads rolling across the floor and winking
he paces the cell all night, demands to know
    if I think his pregnant girlfriend still wants to be with him
one with Marfan Syndrome I call him Big Chief
I call him Frankenstein
    arson, murder, aggravated assault, rape, burglary,
    armed robbery
all together in the special needs block
    at night through the walls the muffled sound of
    flushing power toilets
like blowtorches being lit, cell mates taking shits
right in front of you,
    the snoring, the rustle from masturbation on the bunk
    above you
the misspelled graffiti, the seventeen swastikas
scratched into steel
    the howls from somewhere to the left or the right, people
always gone in the morning, replaced by the guy who keeps to
himself,
    makes no eye contact, wears the green sleeveless poncho
of those on suicide watch, we walk around in the morning
    like overgrown Oompa-Loompas with goatees searching
for the glass elevator, waiting for nothing in the barren room,
    threadbare boxers and socks worn for days,
    fights over the washer and dryer
tap of the CO's baton on the door during headcount,
    the scream from someone maced or tazed for a cookie
    smuggled from lunch

the constant cell searches, and always the card games
in the evening
    gambling away sweet and low, tomorrow's cream of wheat
    or noodles
once a guy begged for candy so much that they stuck pieces up
their assholes
    and gave it to him wrapped, filled a cup of noodles
    with semen
and laughed while the guy crippled with scoliosis
in a wheelchair ate it
    a handful of kids studying GED workbooks, another group
watching "Cops" on the TV, singing together the theme song
    toothbrushes scraped all night against the cement floor
    to make a shiv[1]
ball point pens hollowed and rigged with rubber
from their worn orange deck shoes
    to make a syringe with needles stolen from medical
methadone or dispensed oxycontin burned down
and shot between the toes
    the 'Nam vet telling me he can handle anything but benzos
    they make him crazy
popped for pulling right up next to an ATM,
painting the camera black
    taking a cut saw to the cash box, the light flickering off
    plastic shrapnel
and the pay phone and its short steel vertebrae cord,
the operator
    announcing each time your children answer
    "this call is from an inmate"
and the guards with their rubber gloves, so they don't
touch you
    the guard with one bad eye who makes you walk
    to the left

the guard who gives out fireball candy
    the guard who locks you down for days for laughing
    too loud
the female guard who hits hard with her baton
to show the men she belongs
    the guard who talks about drunken binges, puking
    so hard an eye vessel burst
the guard who barely sleeps,
    the guard who dozes through the night
the guard who asks if he scares me with a thin smile
    and all the old nurses in their frumpy smocks trying
    to get everyone's meds right
avoiding another lawsuit because the admin screams
    not to let another get hep C from blood on the table
the flicker of tongues towards her to show you swallowed
    and when you get used to making the hard shots
    from the back
of the brickyard into the netless hoop
    when the food becomes more edible, even the beans
when you've mastered rolling up your pants for the shower
to not get them wet
    your flip flops slipping untouched through the leg holes
they come for you and walk you out to intake past the trustees
    mopping the floors and showers, past where they
    strip-searched you,
raise the boys, squat and cough, where they took your clothes
and rancid sneakers
    that they now give back, your check from
    the commissary balance
buzz you out into the morning light, trees tinged with red
at the top in September
    smell of fresh cut grass, smell of fresh air, smell of fresh air
    exquisite simple freedom
the clouds, the clouds looking just like clouds
    in the half-remembered expanse of morning sky

the sun a red wax seal on a blue and white envelope
containing instructions for the rest of your careless,
structured days...

[1]Slang for any sharp instrument used as a weapon.

Kurt and MaryTucholsky
Allen Forrest

R.F. Grant

THE MAN IN THE MIRAGE

ON A BRIGHT SPRING DAY, more than a decade ago, two strangers knocked on the other side of Anna Valen's door. Like clockwork, they came at the precise minute the woman sat for an early supper.

Curious, Anna rose. She wove through several rooms, before answering the door.

No one had visited her in over three years.

On the other side of the door, a Japanese man and Caucasian woman stood. Fully suited in business attire, they were poised and upright, still as mannequins. A million particles of dust floated in the afternoon light between them. The woman wore a starched skirt and blouse, both checkered, the Japanese man, a suit of an opposing pale-amber. A dove-shaped pin—opalescent as pearl—sat dead-center above each of their hearts.

Anna opened the door.

Analytical as lab scientists, the two ogled her through their spectacles.

"Name," the man said—pronounced, rather, as if proclaiming a one-word sermon.

"Anna Valen," the Caucasian woman replied. She jotted onto a clipboard, her movements deft as a line assemblyman's.

"Eyes."

The woman veered closer, a nose's length away.

"Light-hazel. Green at center."

Again, the jotting.

"Hair."

"Ash-blonde."

"Body?"

The woman paused. Her lips quivered into the slightest smile.

"Like a tall glass of champagne," she said. The man didn't laugh. Not even a smile. He remained as stoic as a member of the Queen's Guard.

The woman continued writing, finishing at the bottom of the page with a swinging signature. Finally, she glanced at Anna over her glasses.

"Well, it's certainly you," she said. "Do you know why we've come, Miss Valen?"

"I-I don't," Anna said.

The strangers' heads cocked.

"You've been nominated," the man said.

"Nominated, you say? For what?"

"She hasn't been nominated, Hattori. Her—"

"You're right. Her town has. Regardless, you are the reason for its nomination, Miss Valen. We're here to announce the arrival of our auction."

"—the auction of mirages," the woman added.

Little did Anna know, a third stranger had arrived in town merely an hour ago. In a carriage drawn by two horses, the fellow bobbed into the town center, stopping beneath the bell tower. Upon closer observation, the wheels of his carriage seemed imperfect. They weren't entirely round and gave off a gelatinous appearance when spun, bouncing their contents to and fro. Even the gaps between the spokes seemed irregular.

The carriage overflowed with trunks—rectangular ones with half-cylindrical tops, trunks of an oriental antiquity piled atop one another, each having a lock thicker than an alligator's hide.

Perhaps these new arrivals were much-needed. The people of Anna's town had spiraled long ago into the lengthy, abject days of boredom, typical to the desert town in which they lived. Each day dawdled into the next, the hand upon the clock-tower seemingly struggling in a jar of molasses. This was a town where gossip was stirred up by the cedar-and-carob-colored rattlesnakes that snuck into the bedrooms of newborns. This was a place where gas station attendants, their faces resigned, their movements dry and creaking, snapped their suspenders hourly, so as to remove the dust which caked their clothing. Granted, this was a sluggish place, but on a single day, in a matter of hours, something changed.

The carriage came to a halt. Its ebony horses spewed vapor like living steam engines, the exertion of their travels obvious. Their muscles were corded like twisted tree trunks.

They gleamed like panthers in moonlight.

The man driving the carriage sighed before stepping down. He proceeded towards the carriage's backside, keys jingling on his belt loop, before removing a sign.

Propped atop Main Street for all to see, the sign read "The Auction of Mirages" in loopy, oversized paint.

Ancel—as we now know him—began his announcements like a seasoned paper boy. "To witness the mirage is to see the world! Come! Come and see!"

Quiet figures drew near the windows of every building. They stared out upon the foreigner, like animals hiding in a forest alcove and observing a passing predator. The head of every man, woman, and child was crowded behind the dirt-encrusted panes. Eyes showed worry from what sibling ears had heard, and yet no one dared step outside.

Chin held high, Ancel continued his pitch.

"I have attained the emerald heights of Machu Picchu, lain eyes upon snowy villages of Tibet, shaken hands with the *sadhus* of Varanasi, harpooned whales with tribes from the Arctic. Some of you may ask if I've returned empty-handed? Nay, brother and sister. Nay, guardian and child. I've returned with treasures from every part, for all to see and claim."

The people of the town stood entranced by his magniloquence. Intrigue grew like climbing vines in the psyche, swarming over the conscience of every citizen. Chatter escalated between neighbors. Whispers rose with giddy impatience.

Ancel, of course, heard every bit. He listened, cupped hand to ear, waiting for bidders to emerge. After all—one never resisted a mirage, and the minds of Anna's town were thirsty.

Anna herself soon joined the crowd. She and the townspeople turned toward the carriage, watching while the three strangers dragged out every trunk. The luggage thudded onto the dirt, rounded billows of dust puffing out from each trunk.

Finally, all thirty trunks stood stacked in neat orientation around Ancel. The final step was the pedestal.

Ancel was sweating. Despite his lanky attributes, he was a short man. The pedestal, however, made him appear proud and established, when he sold his treasures.

In front of his keepsakes, he set a gilded box. Thereupon he stepped, puffing out his chest.

When he turned back around, all two-hundred citizens had crowded before him, as if silently waiting for a be-heading.

"Shall we begin?" he said.

The largest trunk was brought to the forefront. Ancel removed the key-ring from his belt and unlocked it.

Citizens huddled close, their eyes wide like saucers, their palms itching for gold.

There it lay, the first treasure.

Anna saw it with the rest of her peers: a gold-leafed swan, jewel-encrusted, no larger than a cat. It glittered ethereally from what light lingered in the day.

Anna pictured herself as the owner of this golden swan. How it would renew the decorative beauty of her home, reverse age into innocence again, cause her to speak from lips lily-white.

As she pondered the swan, she looked around. Only women's hands had risen into the air. The men hadn't joined in with the bidding.

The swan eventually went to an elderly, white-haired woman. Her eyes held a look of craving—a yearning for things lost and memories regained. She, a widow to the world.

The bidding increased. More and more hands shot up into the air.

Anna knew her people had almost no money and were coughing up what little they had left. She failed to understand the intrigue of the auction before her. She grimaced, her heart sinking into perilous depths.

The thought of being swindled, of being tricked, consumed her, but Anna kept silent. She intuited that intervention would be meaningless.

The second treasure emerged—a polished crown. Diamonds lined the headpiece, royal spikes blooming into a Fleur-de-Lis. The object radiated power.

Anna felt the desire to bow before it, to kiss the feet of its wearer.

Her townspeople felt the same. They raised their hands to bid, eyes glued upon the treasure, minds obsessed with the patriarchal influence it'd bring them.

When the bidding ceased, the crown had been earned by a middle-aged man. His eyes were abyssal, his black hair bent in all directions.

The most intriguing item of all was the third keepsake. Even Anna couldn't imagine how Ancel and his associates could part with it. It was a pyramid of gold bars, perfectly stacked. Solid gold, they smoldered with a hearty light, even as the sun faded behind the hills. All one-hundred-and-twenty citizen hands shot into the air. Every man, woman, and child desired what they saw.

Only Anna remained still. She kept her hands at her side.

The occasional, paranoid eye shifted her way, because of her refusal to bid, but something within Anna knew better.

The bars went to a young teen. All the potential in the world was laid at his feet, though his eyes were deep-blue pools of fear. He gathered the chest into his arms, hugging it close, as if it would shield him from worldly harm to come.

Dusk bled into the surrounding sky.

Many more items were sold, and all were purchased with great enthusiasm. These were Oriental treasures, prized items from centuries ago—muskets and jewelry, statues and paintings—a history behind each. Not until the very last item appeared, however, did great confusion spark.

One trunk—the smallest of all—came to the crowd's attention. As it did so, Ancel the auctioneer made a proposition. His voice silenced the crowd.

"This last trunk—" he theatrically proposed "—is a paradox."

The faintest glimmer twinkled in his eyes.

The Japanese man continued, "As per auction ruling, it goes to the highest bidder. But there is a condition, you see. One single condition which separates it from the rest."

Ancel turned his head toward the Japanese man and his female associate. Both nodded back at him.

"One cannot know what lies inside until after it has been bought," Ancel finished.

Several seconds passed. Reticence swept over the crowd. No one lifted a finger. Not even a hand. No one except for Anna.

The entire community gasped. Anna found herself a magnet for craning heads. Stares reared her way, as if she'd committed an atrocious crime.

"I will buy it," she affirmed, though she couldn't believe how loudly she spoke.

Ancel stood, completely unphased. He bowed humbly in her direction.

"We have a buyer, then."

Throughout the auction, Ancel had not personally carried a single item to its buyer. This one, he did.

The Japanese man and his female associate looked on.

Gloved hands tucked beneath, Ancel brought the mysterious trunk to Anna and presented it to her. The exchange felt airy, surreal, and an emptiness—there was an emptiness waiting to be filled.

"In which do you believe, Miss Valen?" Ancel finally asked her. All eyes in town studied Anna's face. "—Do you believe in the world? Or do you believe in the illusion?"

Anna shook her head. The question felt more important than all of the treasures sold that day. She didn't know the answer. She couldn't. No one in the entire world could. But an answer surfaced in that moment—the only answer. The right answer.

"Both," she said.

A deadened quiet followed. After what seemed an eternity—a perpetual eternity—a smile warmed Ancel's face. Wisdom slept behind his eyes, he a sage parading as a fool, but Anna had caused the light to awaken.

Tears welled up in his eyes. Ever so simply, he nodded.

In the silence that followed, Anna crept away from the crowd.

Every pair of eyes watched her, though nobody moved to follow her. Not even the Japanese man and the Caucasian woman.

A wind whispered through the town, creaking the framework of boutiques and saloons, lifting the dresses of wives and daughters. A bonnet flew off of somebody's head, joining a passing tumbleweed. A dust-devil pirouetted in the valley nearby.

To it all, Anna turned away. She went home and shut her door. A last envelope of light receded into her room.

A new day awaited. A new world. One of both ash and flourishing life. One of doves singing to rising dawns, fires burning away the horizon.

No one heard from Miss Anna Valen again. She left the dusty town of her birth behind, that desert town with its polished crown; its jeweled swans, oil paintings, and beautiful treasures; its gold bars and observant people, clinging to what piles of material goods they had left.

Not one of the townspeople followed in her footsteps. Not one of them changed in mind.

Only Ancel followed, Ancel and his auction.

In the distance, the mirage of life shimmered. It shimmered and waned, waiting.

Linda Swanberg

GRAHAM THOMAS ROSES

With the drawing of this love and the voice of this calling...
                    —T. S. Eliot, *Four Quartets*

dawn mist over Mt. Sentinel
I take off my slippers, walk on wet grass

Graham Thomas roses open
I bury my face in deep tea-scented cups

cradle yellow blossoms in my hands
petals slip through my fingers like wind—

curl on soaked ground—darken—
love exacts a heavy sweetness from dying

before November snows
I prune green canes, mound crowns with soil

Graham Thomas roses overwinter in my mind
blushed petals timeless as any body

Sameer Joshi

THE TRASHCAN

INVISIBLE MAN

What I am looking for is a life without sham, a place where my bodies—emotional, physical, spiritual—are silent; where they do not get agitated or act up—conjuring fears and solutions, suffering and palliatives, which I could call, for want of a better word, material realities.

So, I have shed my bodies, as my path progressed. I slowly gave up my bodies, and now I exist in a disembodied state, as pure voice. And with all these bodies, I have shed my stories. I wish I had something for you, but I have no stories for you. Not even my own. Do I disappoint you?

TRASHCAN

Silence.

INVISIBLE MAN

You know, it was easy to give up my stories and bodies. The problem now is this gnawing feeling of loss, the feeling that there are stories out there, stories with selves for me to occupy; that there, over the horizon, are places in the light with stories unfolding, though I am missing from them. Are there any such places? Am I right in thinking this way?

Streaks of light arrange themselves in the semblance of a giant face. The pale face glows, his half-smile of satiety frozen, undisturbed, and silent.

INVISIBLE MAN

I often dream I hear voices, promising pleasure and success, goals and destinations, temptations and bliss. I hear them saying, "Come, taste this, be this, be us, occupy us, want us." It is all really so silly, and perhaps I have been down those roads before; but the longer I shun these voices, the more morose I feel. Where is the destination I set out for? Any clues, Housefly?

The housefly buzzes faintly, flying in circles around the giant, glowing face.

INVISIBLE MAN

But all said and done, I can't complain. I like my existence. My bodies were burdens, leading me down dangerous paths. Of course, I assume this was so, for I have no memories, since I gave up my mind. It is now most pleasant to think almost nothing, to feel almost nothing, and to want almost nothing. Excuse me, I need to relax.

LUMINOUS FACE

Almost nothing. The key word is *almost.* Do you know that there are places in the observable universe where the temperature is almost absolute zero; that there are places so distant from any matter or galaxies that almost no light reaches them; that from these places, it is impossible to discern whether there is anything in the universe at all, because all the stuff of the universe is so distant it might as well not exist? And still, enough starlight reaches these places to raise the temperature two degrees above absolute zero. Nowhere in the universe is there freedom from *almost*.

Why, we could be in a place like that, now. I don't see a single thing here except the four of us—sorry, three, for Invisible Man is invisible —and it is cold. If not for the pale warmth of my glow, Housefly would freeze.

The housefly buzzes a little louder, but continues his revolutions at the same pace.

TRASHCAN

You assume that the universe exists. Well, let me tell you something. What is the universe but the story of its unfolding? And what happens to all stories? They end up in the trash, or to be precise, in the Trashcan.

I feel full of trash, even though I am lying on my side. Don't you think it is possible that the universe, or the story of the universe, has been crumpled, shredded, and shoved inside me?

In that case, there is no universe out there. I contain it within me.

Perhaps, if something were to kick me, the story of the universe would spill out and start up again, and it would be populated by sentient beings, who will wonder where the universe came from, where it is going, and what its nature is. They may even realize that it is all garbage.

(Assuming what I say is true, there is still nothing around to kick me strongly enough, and so my claims must remain untested. I am only ruminating and not boasting, so the non-attestable nature of my claim does not bother me in the least.)

All those voices that Invisible Man claims to hear, perhaps they issue from within me, because the real and imaginary selves he mentions shedding have ended up in the trash, that is, in me; though this notion displeases me, because I claim to be certifiably airtight, leak-resistant, and built to last.

HOUSEFLY

Flim-flam. Stories unfold in time, and they need time. If all stories were finished, there wouldn't be any time left.

Since I am flying around these streaks of light—this luminous face— at a regular speed, which is distance divided by time, there is proof enough that time and stories are not totally over. Maybe they are *almost* over, but not yet totally over.

By flying 'round and 'round at a regular rate, I am keeping time alive, for my flying is evidence of time. It is possible that I, the only moving object in the universe or what's left of it, am the reason time still continues.

LUMINOUS FACE

Yes, yes, and since reality needs an observer to confirm itself as reality, I am here. I am the observer which makes this universe real. Aren't we a merry bunch, confirming and supporting each other. It is quite touching.

INVISIBLE MAN

If I were visible, you would see me yawn. What manner of reasoning is this? Either the universe exists, or it doesn't. Has the Trashcan swallowed it whole, or has he *almost* swallowed it? This almost-ness, this unsatisfying incompleteness, tempting itself to unspool into full-fledged being, is the same as full-fledged deception. I have abandoned so much; why won't this almost-ness of things leave me also? What is it within me that doesn't let go these last remnants of the lie?

LUMINOUS FACE

I am too satisfied to attempt a reply.

TRASHCAN

I am sealed. No information escapes me.

HOUSEFLY

I'm just a housefly.

INVISIBLE MAN

If I had an emotional body left, I would be bristling with indignation. What I am tired of, most of all, is the puerile question of beginnings and endings, as if that question were the key to anything; for, properly speaking, the end of something is the beginning of something else and is therefore, the beginning of things. This circling is tiresome.

Even more than that, what I disapprove of—in another era I might have said "despise"—in myself is this desire to seek answers from without, to seek confirmation from another. Insofar as one's external reality is a reflection of one's relationship to one's self, the three of you may well exist completely within me: The Trashcan is a repository for all that I wish to forget, the Luminous Face is the face of my complacency, and the Housefly is the part of me that is enslaved, condemned to keep my story circling the same unmoving point.

If this be the case, I need to be careful. I need to approach each of you three by turns. You first, Luminous Face with that unmoving smile. What is the reason for your mirth in the face of suffering?

It has been my sole motivation to seek transcendence by escaping suffering—the intrigues and conspiracies within and among my bodies; the battles, these constant strikes and counter-strikes; the battles with other bodies; the incompletion of all resolutions; the endless settling of scores; the births and deaths and rebirths—such constant tumult—the pain of birth and the pain of cremation pyres, millions of times.

LUMINOUS FACE

After all has been seen, analyzed, and understood, what remains is a gentle mirth. Your strivings, lofty though they seem to you, are humorous. You climb one foot and slide back two feet. The caricatures of your goals, the frustrating almost-attainment, the almost-ness of it all and then the cycling back to the same quest again and again—What is there not to produce this mirth?

You are at war with your own existence, while secretly being in love with it. You seek to transcend it, and yet long to preserve it. You bring yourself into a state of almost-transcendence on purpose.

You say that you want to escape suffering? See how you embrace suffering with one arm, while shoving it off with another. How deeply you are immersed in your bodies, even as you claim to hate them. You bristle with memories, even as you feign amnesia. You torment yourself with sufferings that you hold close, while crying out for the sufferings to stop.

What a caricature of liberation have you made for yourself—an effigy of disembodied consciousness. The funniest thing of all is that you know your error, your quixotic quests that end in this almost-ness, this almost-completion. What is there not to laugh about?

INVISIBLE MAN

You say I am in love with suffering, but what have I not done to escape it? I have cycled through life after life, seeking teachings, clues, paths, and methods. I have drawn myself above the corporeal, the emotional, and the spiritual. I have known states of hell and states of bliss. I have labored to drop everything that could be the ground for suffering, have I not?

TRASHCAN

It is impossible to escape everything. Everything you say you have abandoned lies safe within me, ready to spring up and devour you again in a moment. It is all locked up and safe.

HOUSEFLY

And where there is trash, there are flies. I, the Housefly, am the tiny buzzing sound of your self-betrayal; the tiny part of you that wants to start up the drama again; the secret love you have for your bodies and stories; their bliss and their pains, the mesmerizing saga of your existence.

The fly continues to buzz. The semblance of a face formed by the streaks of light smiles.

INVISIBLE MAN

I cycled through existences. I found love and then discovered it was deceit. I sought to belong and had to stomach banishment. I sought knowledge and found chicanery. I sought truth and found palaver. I sought my own self and discovered only the hollow echo of other voices. I was weary and sad and afraid.

I gave myself to a lofty pursuit. I refined myself until none of my bodies was left, for what is the fruit of existence? This existence causes one to suffer. It smites and deludes, constantly. It keeps one from knowledge and repeats itself in cycles, keeping one lashed to the wheel of *karma*.

I sought to rid myself of all that suffering could latch on to. I am now a dot of consciousness. At least, this is what I think must have happened, for I have no memory anymore.

HOUSEFLY

Why, you are such a bore. May I sing? Singing does help with boredom.

Housefly begins a tuneless humming atop his buzzing.

TRASHCAN

Don't sing at the invisible man's misfortunes. Can't you see how he has suffered?

LUMINOUS FACE

True. His story is touching.

TRASHCAN

In fact, his story is heartbreaking.

The trashcan and the streaks of light in the semblance of a face muffle their laughter. Then, they laugh aloud, trying to speak, but failing.

TRASHCAN

As you know, Invisible Man, I am the repository of the detritus known as the universe. I contain records of its doings. I contain the discarded reels of all the movies your species has enjoyed.

These movies are made up of celluloid. The celluloid contains pigments that turn into colors, when exposed to light. Little dots of color are suspended in celluloid. It is quite pretty.

The point I am making is this. There are happy movies and sad movies, movies filled with mirth and movies filled with suffering; but looking into the celluloid, all is no more than a wonder-world of colored dots. There is no inherent joy or pain in the dots of pigment. Where is this suffering you talk about?

INVISIBLE MAN

I am talking not of the play of light and shadow, of celluloid and pigment, but of actual existence—

LUMINOUS FACE

What is the big difference? Isn't existence a story also, a tale you tell yourself by making something out of nothing?

INVISIBLE MAN

You are mistaken, for you equate the play of light and shadow upon a screen with real existence. The movie ends in a few hours, but existence resumes itself, lifetime after lifetime.

LUMINOUS FACE

You do get immersed in movies, do you not? Don't you quake at the ghost, horripilate at the suspense, fall in love with the actor, and weep at the tragedy? I say that, at the level of response, there is no difference between your existence and the movie. Existence is just a movie, with each lifetime a longer and longer reel. Don't you think so?

TRASHCAN

(*Laughing*) Don't talk to him of trivial things like movies. Can't you see he is almost enlightened?

LUMINOUS FACE

Oh, hush.

TRASHCAN

(*Stammering*) No, what I meant was that the pixels in celluloid—

INVISIBLE MAN

How can you compare a movie to actual existence? While we watch a movie, we may weep, but we know we are watching a movie. This is not true in real life. As the Trashcan says, one is trivial, and one is real.

LUMINOUS FACE

Who says movies are trivial? Had stories been trivial, your species would not have been telling them every chance it got. No, stories are real. The difference is this. You take the story of what you call your real life not to be a story.

INVISIBLE MAN

But I never hurt, while I am watching a movie, as I have in real life.

LUMINOUS FACE

That is because you are not watching but playing a character in what you call reality. Your bodies will experience the pain, as if it were real.

INVISIBLE MAN

While I watch a movie, I know it is a creation of a certain agent. What is real existence by comparison? Who would create this sad lot, where I and others like me drag our defeated lives behind us, lamenting our sufferings?

LUMINOUS FACE

You assume that the material world is separate from consciousness and that consciousness creates the material world, but there is no separation. The material world, gross or subtle, is only a face of consciousness. You and everything you experience are but tendrils of consciousness. Consciousness is the author of everything, the substance of everything, the source of all color and taste and scent and touch, the beginning of all stories and their end. Consciousness exults in its powers. You are not separate from consciousness, even in your most gross material form. You are consciousness.

INVISIBLE MAN

But then, why suffering? If consciousness is the supreme storyteller, why are the stories filled with suffering?

LUMINOUS FACE

Why not? What kind of storyteller would write a story where everything is pleasant and blissful, where the bliss does not swing into all possible extremes, where there is not pain as well as pleasure? If a story were lacking these, it would be flat and bland, and the audience would reject it.

The forest requires all types of trees to exist—the thorny tree and the fruiting tree. It needs all animals—the benign ones and the dangerous ones. You are a character in the forest. You will feast on sweet fruit and also step on thorns. You will laugh, and you will hurt. You will live a life filled with extremes.

You think these extremes are the problem, but they are not. Take away the extremes and all you are left with is a flat plane of nothingness. You return to this flat plane periodically when you die, but consciousness is an ever-shifting kaleidoscope, and no sooner do you die than you are born again, bearing the costumes and colors and predilections that your *karma* has determined.

You will experience exalted lives, mean lives, and ordinary lives. All this is the play of consciousness.

INVISIBLE MAN

If what you say is so, then what is wrong with seeking an elevated life? What is wrong with entering subtle realms, free of one's bodies?

LUMINOUS FACE

By itself, there is nothing wrong with seeking such a life. You can attain blissful states using your spiritual powers. There are heavens, where all is music and dance and feasting. You can enter these heavens. You can enter realms of wisdom, where all is righteousness and purity. If you wish, there are hellish realms where all is violence, deceit, putrefaction, and immorality—where the inhabitants live on each other's flesh. You can go where you please, but sooner or later, your spiritual merit or demerit runs out and you end up where you started, in the glorious mud and muck of embodied existence.

You have experienced this. You have realized this. You deceive yourself again and again, pretending to forget this.

You moan, "I suffer, I suffer," and you set up all manners of charades to help yourself: routines, religions, cults, highways and byways to liberation, contortions of mind and body, abstinence.

"I shall not be wrathful," you claim, and you go around like the cartoon of an unruffled ship.

"I shall be pure and above the reach of sensuality," you proclaim, and off you go, looking like another cartoon of chastity.

Sometimes, you succeed, attaining subtle forms at the experience of gross ones, but your success is illusory; for in battling material existence, you are at battle with consciousness itself. The gross material world is a manifestation of consciousness.

Only by being fully existent, only by taking the bull of that existence by the horns and staring into its deep black eyes, will you see yourself in those eyes, reflected as consciousness itself—as consciousness in which all states, realms, bodies, thoughts, feelings, sensations and stories are included; for they all derive from it, return to it, are it.

INVISIBLE MAN

What then of the cults of embodiment, those that make an obsession of the body—feeding it, housing it, adorning it, satisfying its appetites, creating appetites where there were none? You know, the opposite of abstinence?

LUMINOUS FACE

Both the cult of abstinence and the cult of indulgence are ignorant of the true nature of existence. The two see the body as separate from consciousness: The former seeks to elevate the self out of the realm of the body and into the realm of consciousness, while the latter turns the body into a fetish, as if afraid of what might lie beyond it. Both schools of thought fear the death of the body: The former seeks release from the material body prior to physical death, while the latter primps the body to stave off death as long as it can.

But death is nothing to be afraid of. It is only the mutation of one body into another. Acceptance of death entails no rejection of the body, no demand to stop nurturing physical form, but only the acceptance of death as a holy fact, a beautiful fact—the pod bursting open in the sun to scatter its seed, and then floating away as husk.

Nobody speaks for a long time. Only the fly continues to sing and buzz.

HOUSEFLY

Trash. Everything is trash. There is nothing to learn, Invisible Man. There is no teaching for you here.

INVISIBLE MAN

But there is. What you have taught me is that I must neither indulge nor escape the body. Indulging the body is born from ego, while trying to escape embodied existence by entering loftier realms is a desire born from a higher form of ego. You have taught me that both approaches are doomed.

You have taught me that my salvation lies in squarely facing embodied existence, while realizing that existence is only an expression of consciousness; that states and moods, elevated or depressed, pleasant or painful, lifetimes exalted or lowly—all these simply pass across the face of consciousness, as do colored leaves on the surface of a stream, or images projected onto a movie screen.

You have taught me to seek myself as the consciousness across which everything flows, as the consciousness that takes on myriad forms while remaining itself unaffected as the root, as the source that dreams all forms.

I am now ready to return to embodied existence—to taste the fruiting tree with my tongue, to feel the rocks under my soles, to drink the water filtered through moss. I am ready to realize myself through embodied existence, and for this I have you to thank.

LUMINOUS FACE

You have only yourself to thank. You inquired into your own self, and you have received the answer. I have told you what you already knew, for I exist only in your own consciousness. Now, you are ready to enter your present lifetime. This timekeeper, this housefly, has lived out his usefulness.

HOUSEFLY

No, no, don't you dare!

The housefly buzzes louder and flies faster, but the luminous face suddenly extends his tongue. The fly sticks to it, and the tongue withdraws. The buzzing stops. The luminous face smiles. The face and the trashcan begin to circle the invisible man, so fast that they became a blur. The luminous face laughs loudly. The trashcan bursts open. Then, all around, galaxies light up, spinning 'round and 'round. The invisible man feels his bodies enveloping him again, as he gets caught up in the whirling color, spinning and returning in the midst of a mad rainbow.

CONTRIBUTOR NOTes

JOEL ALLEGRETTI is the author of four collections of poetry, most recently *Europa/Nippon/New York: Poems/Not-Poems* (Poets Wear Prada, 2012). He is also the editor of *Rabbit Ears* (Poets Wear Prada, 2014), the first anthology of poetry about television. His work has appeared in the *New York Quarterly, Barrow Street, Smartish Pace*, and other national journals, as well as in journals published in Canada, the United Kingdom, Belgium, and India.

GUY R. BEINING has had six poetry books and five chapbooks published over the years. He has also appeared in seven different anthologies. Recent publications include *Chain, Ep;phany, Perspektive, New Orleans Review*, and the *New Review of Literature*.

LISA BELLAMY is the author of *Nectar* (Encircle Publications, 2011) and teaches at the Writers Studio. Her writing has appeared in *Triquarterly*, the *Sun, Massachusetts Review, New Ohio Review*, and the *Southampton Review*, among other publications. In 2008, she won the Fugue Poetry Prize. Bellamy practices with the Tergar Meditation Community and, with her husband, is a member of St. Bartholomew's Episcopal Church in New York City.

RICHARD ALAN BUNCH is a three-time Pushcart Prize nominee and the author of several collections of poetry, including *Greatest Hits: 1970-2000* (Pudding House, 2001), *Wading the Russian River* (Norton Coker Press, 1993), and *Running for Daybreak* (Edwin Mellen Press, 2004). His poetry has appeared in *Windsor Review, Poetry New Zealand, Hurricane Review, Poem, Hawai'i Review, Many Mountains Moving, Red River Review, Slant, Homestead Review, Dirigible, Haight Ashbury Literary Journal, West Wind Review, Comstock Review,* and the *Oregon Review.* His latest work is titled *Zen Sight and Tangerine Butterflies: New and Selected Poems* (Infinity Publishing, 2014). He resides with his family in Davis, California.

MICHAEL CADMUS is a recent graduate of Montclair State University. His poems have appeared in the *Idiom* and *Emerge Literary Magazine.* He is currently a high school English teacher in New Jersey.

RICH CAMPBELL has stolen the Psalms LPs from the Riverland College library in Austin, Minnesota, where he teaches English and Humanities. He holds a Ph.D. in American Literature, sometimes thinks stones should be carved into pictures, and (many days of his recent life) dotes on his son Nicholas. His hearing and eyes aren't what they used to be, there are irons twisting in the fires, and his yellow dog is slowly dying—so he's become much more interested in seeing and listening. His poems have appeared in *Poetic Strokes, Crossings at Carnegie Poet/Artist Collaboration,* and the juried poet/photography book, *Open to Interpretation: Intimate Landscape* (Open to Interpretation, 2012).

RUTH ANN DANDREA writes fiction, poetry, and nonfiction. Her writings have recently appeared in *Mean for Tea, Quiddity, Thema, Doubly Mad,* and the *Bitter Oleander.* She is the author of a chapbook, *Elemental* (Black Rabbit Press, 2014)

GLORIA DYC serves as Regents' Professor of English at the University of New Mexico-Gallup, where she meets the needs of under-prepared native students. She currently practices Tibetan Buddhism with the Venerable Bhakha Tulku Rinpoche of the Nyingmapa School. He is the fifth reincarnation of a disciple of Padmasambava; the latter introduced the teachings of Buddha to Tibet. She is the author of *200 New Mexico Poems* (The UNM Press, 2014). Her work has recently appeared in *Gargoyle #59,* as well as the online publications *BRICKrhetoric 2013* and *Between the Lines.*

LAURA EKLUND lives and writes in Olive Hill, KY with her husband George Eklund, who is also a writer. They are both professors. Find out more about her at http://www.lauraeklund.org or follow her on Facebook at The Art of Laura Eklund.

Graphic artist and painter ALLEN FORREST was born in Canada and bred in the U.S. He has created cover art and illustrations for literary publications and books. He is the winner of the Leslie Jacoby Honor for Art at San Jose State University's *Reed Magazine* and his *Bel Red* painting series is part of the Bellevue College Foundation's permanent art collection. Forrest's expressive drawing and painting style is a mix of Avant-Garde Expressionism and Post-Impressionist elements, reminiscent of van Gogh.

KATHY FRENCH is a retired Professor from Utah Valley University. Her interest in peace and justice is strengthened by collecting an oral history of peace activists in Utah, recalling her experiences in Uganda, and being a member of the Quaker faith. Kathy is happily a vagabond in the American West. www.facebook.com/kathy.french.927

LARRY E. GRAHAM lives and works in Sacramento, CA. His stories have appeared in *Descant*, *Straylight*, *Avalon Literary Review*, the *Listening Eye*, and *Susurrus*. His current project is a short story cycle about people who live in a rooming house.

R.F. GRANT is an author of fiction and non-fiction. He was a Top 10 Finalist in the 2014 *TIFERET: A Journal of Spiritual Literature's* International Writing Contest. Mr. Grant has been published in such journals as the YSU Student Literary Arts Association's *Jenny Magazine*, the *Cold Mountain Review*, *Gravel Magazine: The University of Arkansas' MFA Literary Journal*, *Ruminate Magazine*, and others. His work has been described as magical-realist and spiritual, as well as deeply sentimental towards the human experience. His writing has also been noted as thematically-similar to Gabriel Garcia Marquez, Paulo Coelho, Khaled Hosseini, and Salman Rushdie. For more information, visit www.rfgrant.com.

KATHLEEN GUNTON began publishing poetry and photography after graduating from California State University, Long Beach. Her poetry has been published in *Sojourners*, *Perceptions*, and the William Stafford anthology, *A Ritual to Read Together* (Woodley Press, 2013). Her artwork has recently appeared on the covers of *Tiferet*, *Art & Letters*, and *Thema*. Find more images at Kathleen Gunton Blog/Discursion.

KHANH HA is the author of *Flesh* (Black Heron Press, 2012) and *The Demon Who Peddled Longing* (Underground Voices, 2014). He is a three-time Pushcart nominee and the recipient of *Greensboro Review's* 2014 Robert Watson Literary Prize in Fiction. His work has appeared in *Waccamaw Journal*, *storySouth*, *Greensboro Review*, *Permafrost Magazine*, *Saint Ann's Review*, *Moon City Review*, the *Long Story*, *Red Savina Review*, *DUCTS*, *ARDOR*, *Lunch Ticket*, *Cha: An Asian Literary Journal*, *Yellow Medicine Review*, and other fine journals.

JIM HART is the author of *Ramblings of a One-Eyed Garbage Man* (CreateSpace, 2013). His work has been published in more than 45 poetry journals and reviews, and appeared in many countries, including the United States, England, Austria, India, Scotland, Wales, Canada, Germany, New Zealand, and South Africa, as well as on the web.

KELLY JADON is the author of a poetry book, *To Taste the Oil: The Flavor of Life in the Middle East* (Into the Deep Books, 2014). Her poem "To Taste the Oil" was recently featured at the University of Colorado's Eye Contact event as an audible poem. Her poetry has been published both online and in print, in several literary journals. She also writes the syndicated column "Hometown Heroes," which publishes nationally online and locally, in Florida newspapers and magazines. She is a graduate of Spring Arbor University and holds a degree in English, with a concentration on poetry. Find her online at KellyJadon.com.

THOMAS PENN JOHNSON was born in Greensboro, NC on August 22, 1943. He studied Classical Studies, English Literature, English History, and Teaching the Gifted successively at Concordia Senior College at Fort Wayne, the University of North Carolina at Greensboro, Syracuse University, and Wake Forest University. In July 2009, he retired from then-Edison-State-College in Fort Myers, after serving twenty-six years as an instructor of English and humanities. He has published one collection of poems entitled *If Rainbows Promise Not in Vain* (Wyndham Hall Press, 1992).

SAMEER JOSHI is a student in the M.F.A. Creative Writing program at University of Missouri in Kansas City. He also holds a Ph.D. in Film Studies from the University of Kansas. He writes fiction and poetry, and also draws and paints. Some of his art is available at sj-vileen.blogspot.com. "The Trashcan" is his first fiction publication.

MARILYN JOY is a retired teacher of art and English. She has been a dancer, visual artist, writer, and meditator—a seeker and surveyor of new spiritual landscapes. Her poetry has been published in literary journals and magazines, and she has won awards in the National Federation of State Poetry Societies' annual contest.

SARAH KATHARINA KAYß (KAYSS) won the Manuscript Award from the German Writers Association for her poetry and essay collection *Ich Mag Die Welt So Wie Sie Ist* (Allitera, Germany; 2014). She edits a bilingual literary magazine, the *Transnational* (www.the-transnational.com) and is working on her doctorate in military sociology at King's College in London. Her artwork, essays, and poetry have appeared in literary magazines, journals, and anthologies in Germany, Switzerland, Austria, the United Kingdom, Italy, Canada, New Zealand, and the United States.

ELEANOR KEDNEY is the founder of the Writers Studio in Tucson, a branch of the New York-based Writers Studio, and served as the director and advanced workshop teacher for ten years. Her poems have appeared or are forthcoming in *Connecticut River Review*, *Cumberland River Review*, *Many Mountains Moving*, *Miramar Poetry Journal*, *Mudfish*, *NY Quarterly*, *San Pedro River Review*, the *Maynard* and several other journals. Her work appears in the anthologies *No Achilles: War Poetry* (WaterWood Press, 2015) and *Write to Meow* (Grey Wolfe Publishing, 2015). She is also the author of a chapbook, *The Offering* (Liquid Light Press, 2016). She lives with her husband Peter, their dog Charlie, and their cat Ivy in Tucson, AZ and Stonington, CT.

RAY KEIFETZ has published stories and poems in numerous literary journals, including the *Bitter Oleander*, *Kestrel*, *Sand Hill Review*, *Sugar House Review*, and the anthology, *Among Animals* (Ashland Creek Press, 2014), and has received a Pushcart Prize nomination. He lives in Northern California, where he earns his living peddling wine.

ROBERT KOSTUCK is an M.Ed. graduate from Northern Arizona University. Recently published prose appears in *So To Speak*, the *Massachusetts Review*, the *Southwest Review*, *Alimentum*, *Crab Creek Review*, *Event*, *Flyway*, *Saint Ann's Review*, and is forthcoming in *Kenyon Review Online* and *Silk Road*. He is currently working on a novel and living near an ocean. His heart belongs to the Chihuahua and Sonora deserts.

SIMM LANDRES is a native New Yorker, lives in Virginia, and is the father of two. His writings have appeared in *Poem*, *California Quarterly*, *Euphony*, *Snake Nation Review*, and *Little Star*.

W.F. LANTRY is a native of San Diego, CA and received his Ph.D. in Creative Writing from University of Houston. His most recent poetry collection is *The Structure of Desire* (Little Red Tree, 2012), which won a 2013 Nautilus Award in Poetry. He is also the author of *The Language of Birds* (Finishing Line Press, 2011). Recent honors include the National Hackney Literary Award in Poetry, Lindberg Foundation International Poetry for Peace Prize (in Israel), and the Potomac Review Prize. His work appears in *Asian Cha*, *Gulf Coast*, and *Aesthetica*. He currently works in Washington, D.C. and is an associate fiction editor of the online journal *JMWW*.

LYN LIFSHIN has published over 130 books, including three from Black Sparrow Press. Her newest book is *A Girl Goes into The Woods* (NYQ Books, 2013). Her recent books include *Knife Edge & Absinthe: The Tango Poems* (Night Ballet Press, 2012), *All the Poets (Mostly) Who Have Touched Me, Living and Dead, and All True, Especially the Lies* (World Parade Books, 2011), *Ballroom* (March Street Press, 2010), *Barbaro: Beyond Brokenness* (Texas Review Press, 2009), and *The Licorice Daughter: My Year with Ruffian* (Texas Review Press, 2005). Her web site: www.lynlifshin.com

JOHN MCCARTHY'S work has appeared or is forthcoming in the *Minnesota Review*, the *Pinch*, the *Wisconsin Review*, *Oyez Review*, *Salamander*, *Jabberwock Review*, *Midwestern Gothic*, and *Buddhist Poetry Review*, among others. He lives in Chicago, Illinois, where he is the Assistant Editor of *Quiddity: International Literary Journal and Public Radio Program*. He is also a Contributing Editor at Twelve Winters Press, where he edited the anthology *[Ex]tinguished & [Ex]tinct* (Twelve Winters Press, 2014).

ELIZABETH MOLLER is a writer living in New York City. She was named a finalist in *Glimmer Train's* June 2014 Fiction Open contest, and a finalist and runner-up in both the fiction and creative nonfiction categories of the *Pinch's* 2015 literary contests. She was awarded a scholarship to, and participated in, an August 2014 creative writing workshop at the Mayapple Center. This is her first published story.

B.Z. NIDITCH is a poet, playwright, fiction writer, and teacher. His work is widely published in journals and magazines throughout the world, including *Columbia: A Magazine of Poetry and Art*, the *Literary Review*, *Denver Quarterly*, *Hawai'i Review*, *Le Guepard* (France), *Kadmos* (France), *Prism International*, *Jejune* (Czech Republic), *Leopold Bloom* (Budapest), *Antioch Review*, and *Prairie Schooner*, among others. His latest poetry collections are *Lorca at Sevilla* (March Street Press, 2012) and *Captive Cities* (Presa Press, 2012). He lives in Brookline, Massachusetts.

AYAZ DARYL NIELSEN is a husband, father, veteran, x-roughneck (as on oil rigs), and hospice nurse. He is also the editor of *bear creek haiku* (24+ years/120+ issues) bearcreekhaiku.blogspot.com. For this, he thanks his beloved wife/poet Judith Partin-Nielsen and worthy assistant Frosty. His own writing has found homes in *Lilliput Review*, *High Coupe*, *Eye On Life*, *Shamrock*, *SCIFAIKUEST*, and *Shemom*.

ED O'CASEY received his M.A. from the University of North Texas and his M.F.A. from New Mexico State University. His poems have appeared or are upcoming in *Cold Mountain Review*, *Tulane Review*, *Berkeley Poetry Review*, *Euphony*, *Mayo Review*, *Poetry Quarterly*, *NANO Fiction*, and *West Trade Review*. He lives in Wisconsin with his wife and daughter.

HAYA POMRENZE'S poems have appeared or are forthcoming in numerous journals including *Rattle*, *5AM*, *MiPOesias*, and *Lake Effect*, as well as collaborative poems with Denise Duhamel in *Toad* and other journals. Her first book *Hook* (Rock Press, 2007) was nominated for the National Jewish Book Award. Her most recent collection is *How It's Done* (Finishing Line Press, 2014). Haya is an occupational therapist and uses poetry as a healing tool on a psychiatric unit.

ELISAVIETTA RITCHIE'S collections of poetry include *Spirit of the Walrus* (Bright Hill Press, 2005), *Arc of the Storm* (Signal Books, 1998), *Elegy for the Other Woman* (Signal Books, 1996), *Raking the Snow* (Washington Writers Publishing House, 1982), and *Tightening the Circle over Eel Country* (Acropolis Books, 1974). Her fiction books include *In Haste I Write You This Note* (Washington Writers Publishing House, 2000) and others. Ritchie's work is widely published, translated, and anthologized. She writes, teaches, mentors, edits, translates, photographs, and serves as poet-in-the-schools.

MATT SCHUMACHER has published poems in *Cincinnati Review*, the *Fiddlehead*, *Fourteen Hills*, and the *Green Mountain Review 25 Year Poetry Retrospective* issue. He serves as Poetry Editor for a journal of New Fabulism called *Phantom Drift*. His books include *Spilling the Moon* (Wordcraft of Oregon, 2008) and *The Fire Diaries* (Wordcraft of Oregon, 2010).

DAVID SWALLOW, JR. is a traditional Lakota Spiritual Leader and a Head Man of the Lakota Nation. His essay was originally published at www.SilvrDrach.homestead.com. It was edited by Stephanie M. Schwartz, who is a member of the Native American Journalists Association (NAJA).

LINDA SWANBERG received her M.A. from the University of Montana in 1977, and now studies with Tobin Simon, Co-Director of The Proprioceptive Writing Center in Oakland, CA. A lifelong resident of Montana, Linda lives in Missoula with her husband Gregg and one cat "Blu." From her back garden she can track the movement of deer across Mt. Sentinel. Often, deer steal into her garden at night to sleep under the apple trees. Her work has appeared in the *Griffin, HeartLodge, Pennsylvania English, Quiddity International Literary Journal, RE:AL, Riversedge*, the *South Carolina Review, Weber: The Contemporary West*, and elsewhere.

Born within whispering distance of Lake Michigan and riddled by the Grand River, Z.G. TOMASZEWSKI is a rambler and journeyman fresh out of a boat yard and now working in Glacier National Park. Tomaszewski is a founding organizer of Lamp Light Music Festival, as well as a founding member of Great Lakes Commonwealth of Letters, a literary organization based in Grand Rapids, Michigan. His poems have appeared or are forthcoming in publications including *Parabola, Cold Mountain Review, Scintilla, Fogged Clarity, OVS Magazine*, and *Southword Journal*, among others.

WILLIAM VARNER'S work has appeared in *Boston Review*, the *Cincinnati Review*, the *Cimarron Review; Smartish Pace; War, Literature, and the Arts*; and elsewhere. Originally from Pennsylvania, he is lucky to call Maine his home and to work in (the other) Portland, right across the street from Longfellow's childhood home.

BRIAN PHILLIP WHALEN is a doctoral candidate in creative writing at the University at Albany, SUNY. He received his M.F.A. from Iowa State University. His work appears recently or is forthcoming in *Beecher's*, *Blueline*, the *Chattahoochee Review*, *Chautauqua*, *Cream City Review*, *Cutbank*, the *Newer York*, *Pank*, and *Rhino*. He lives in upstate New York with his adorable wife.

LALITAMBA SARANAM

P.O. Box 131, Planetarium Station; New York, NY 10024

Lalitamba partners with Lalitamba Saranam, a holistic homeless shelter in New York City. Through years of working with people in need of permanent housing, we understand how stressful the situation can be. Lalitamba Saranam offers all the comforts of home to women in transition, including survivors of domestic violence, runaway youth, and women with children.

• Social Services

• Life Skills

• Art Studio

• Yoga, Meditation, and Massage

• Clothing Boutique

• Street Outreach

• Soup Kitchen

To make a tax-deductible donation to the shelter, please mail a check to Lalitamba Saranam at the above address. Your generosity makes it all possible. Thank you!

www.threejewelsrefuge.org

SUBSCRIBE

P.O. Box 131, Planetarium Station;
New York, NY 10024

_____$12 One-Year Subscribtion (one annual issue)

_____$20 Two-Year Subscription (two annual issues)

Please include $4.95 for postage and handling and enclose a check written to *Lalitamba*.

Begin my subscription with issue number _____

Name_____

Address_____

City, State, Zip_____

Please send a gift subscription to:

Begin the subscription with issue number _____

Name_____

Address_____

City, State, Zip_____

NEW FROM CHINTAMANI BOOKS

www.chintamanibooks.org

Comfort of the Afflicted: Devotion to Mary
Lalitamba Mandiram
ISBN 978-0-9960236-9-6
Chintamani Books, 2015

Comfort of the Afflicted includes the Blessed Mother's direct words and guidance, a new meditation on the Rosary, traditional Catholic prayers in English and Latin, and contemporary devotions. The book was compiled during the 2015 Lenten season as an offering for prison inmates. It is a call to each of us for repentance, forgiveness, and renewal of heart.

Bhagavad Gita: The Lord's Song
Swamini Sri Lalitambika Devi, Translator
ISBN 978-0-9960236-6-5
Chintamani Books, 2015

A treasure house of wisdom, the *Bhagavad Gita* is said to contain the essence of every *Upanishad*. In conversation with the disciple Arjuna, the Lord reveals wisdom that is as relevant today as it was thousands of years ago— secrets of action, devotion, meditation, and renunciation. This volume contains English and Sanskrit texts. A comprehensive introduction explores the scripture's cultural, historical, and psychological context. The book is an offering to the Lord who lives in your heart.

www.ingramcontent.com/pod-product-compliance
Lightning Source LLC
Chambersburg PA
CBHW031341170626
46807CB00002B/785